W9-ATE-005

The Helping Interview ✢

ALFRED BENJAMIN

University of Tel Aviv
Haifa College
Israel

HOUGHTON MIFFLIN COMPANY

BOSTON *New York Atlanta Geneva, Ill. Dallas Palo Alto*

To the families, sweethearts, and friends of those who gave their lives for their respective countries during the Arab-Israeli Six-Day War of 1967 I dedicate this book with the fervent hope that peace in the Middle East is near and that fruitful cooperation will soon prevail among the nations of the region.

EDITOR'S INTRODUCTION

The interview — a tool or a relationship? The interview — to get or to give, or to be? To trace the history of these meanings is almost to trace the history of counseling, of social work, of medicine in the United States. Certainly the interview literature of thirty years ago stressed the "tool" concept of the interview: to get information about the interviewees that would be useful in hiring employees or in racking up columns of research data. Even in the conduct of the psychiatric interview much probing and interpreting, asking and telling, took place, for the psychiatrist of thirty years ago, who had been recently introduced to psychoanalysis, knew well what he had to do. He was responsible for "finding out" about the patient and then interpreting him to himself. To develop the image of the interview as a tool for probing and operating on the psyche is to exaggerate a bit, but perhaps it is not too far off. Similarly, the social caseworker was there to *get the facts* so that she could make the necessary decisions. And counselors *gathered information* from the student for counselor use.

These uses of the interview are not all malicious, nor are they out of date. The point is that obtaining information was the major purpose of the interview in earlier days but now plays a lesser role. Today the emphasis is heavily upon the "helping" interview, in which the relationship function is stressed. In fact, if we take into account all forms of communication that transpire in the interview, then we see that the interview *is* the relationship. The current need in all kinds of helping professions — school and college counseling, social casework, rehabilitation counseling, much of medicine and psychiatry — is this: to learn *how* to make the interview a helping relationship. There may be some communication of information, but the focus is now upon the growth process in the client. Not all will agree with me, but I believe there must necessarily be a

vii

healthy by-product of growth and change in the *interviewer* as well if the relationship is truly an open and creative one. Thus the objective of the interview is to develop a relationship characterized by mutual trust and creative change.

This book is on just this critical topic of how to make the helping interview a helping relationship. It is the only current book I know about that deals sensitively and totally with *the interview.* The writing is beautifully clear and artistically appealing. The outline is simple enough for a high school graduate to grasp, the thought and wording psychologically profound enough for any specialist in human relations. A great deal of help is skillfully given to both professional and amateur on such vital issues as the use of questions (or better their non-use!), the damage done by the "why" query, the blocking of communication by our own defensive behaviors, etc. If a reader is inclined to underline significant passages in books, he will be troubled here, for every sentence has a peculiar appeal that invites underlining!

I predict a very useful life for this profoundly simple treatment of the kind of helping interviews that thousands of professionals use every day and that thousands of students are preparing to use. Am I allowed as an editor to be enthusiastic? If I am, then I would classify this as a little gem of a book, professionally cut and shaped, with a beautifully polished surface and warm, live lights within.

C. Gilbert Wrenn

PREFACE

Interviewing has occupied much of my thought and time during the past ten years. I have practiced it, taught it, reflected upon it. Now, after much deliberation, I have decided to write about it.

The interview of concern to me is the helping interview. Basically, I suppose, there are two types of interviews: the one in which the interviewer seeks help from the interviewee and the one in which the interviewer tries to help the interviewee. The lines may not always be clear-cut, but the intent of each is clear. The former includes the journalistic interview, research interview, and personnel manager's interview. The journalist wants his story, the researcher his information, the personnel manager the right man for the job vacant at his plant. For them the interview is a tool to assist them in obtaining what they need. If as they apply their skill they help the interviewee as well, this is more or less incidental.

The interview I shall discuss herein is the second kind. Its primary goal is to help the interviewee. He is at the center; he is the focus; he is all-important. Everything else is incidental.

To me an interview is a conversation between two people, a conversation that is serious and purposeful. In the interview the purpose of which is to help the interviewee, he may come to us of his own free will, looking for help. He may come against his will, forced by law or other agents, perhaps even by ourselves. He may come seeking assistance and resenting himself and us for it. Whatever the case may be, the ultimate question for the interviewer must always be: How can I best help this person?

I am not certain I can define "help" satisfactorily to myself. That is, perhaps, one reason for this book. Help is an enabling act. The interviewer enables the interviewee to recognize, to feel, to know, to decide, to choose whether to change. This enabling act demands giving on the part of the interviewer. He must give of his time, his capacity to listen and understand, his skill, his knowledge, his interest — part of himself. If this giving can be perceived by the interviewee, the enabling act will involve receiving. The interviewee will receive the help in a way possible for him to receive it and meaningful to him. The helping interview is the largely verbal interaction between interviewer and interviewee in which this enabling act takes place. It takes place but does not always succeed in its purpose; often we do not know if it has or not.

The helping interview is the kind of conversation in which many people, representing numerous occupations, are engaged much of the time. The doctor is so employed when speaking to his patient, the educator when talking to his pupil. The psychologist, the social worker, the rehabilitation man, the counselor, the placement officer — all these and many others engage in the helping interview when working with their clients. Although they bring with them additional varying skills and backgrounds, they all interview and deeply wish to help. To them these words are addressed. Certainly not because I have all the answers; I know I do not. I don't even know if answers suitable for everyone and every situation exist. My aim is, rather, to stimulate thought and interest — for the first time or afresh — in this aspect of our professional life.

In Israel, where I live and work, I have been teaching interviewing at Tel Aviv University and Haifa College. In the rehabilitation work and personal counseling I have done over the years I have interviewed many people. During my sabbatical year at Temple University in 1967–68, away from daily chores and responsibilities, I put down on paper my approach to and views on the helping interview. Many books on interviewing — and fine ones — already exist. However, those I know of that deal exclusively with the helping interview are few indeed. Much is published for the interview specialist, little for the general practitioner of the art. I feel certain that a basic approach to the helping interview is important to both groups. The former will presumably receive it as part of their professional training. But the latter, who are too often neglected, are the ones for whom my book is particularly meant. What follows is intended for all those who — whether engaged in the helping interview for years or on the threshold of their careers — want to think more deeply about what is involved in the interviewing process and become more aware of their own role, attitudes, and ways of communicating in this important professional task.

The interview extracts cited throughout this book have been compiled from several sources. Some are taken from audio-tapes, others from notes written down during or immediately after interviews. Still others are of my own invention. Many extracts are from interviews conducted by students or colleagues and are used with their permission; others are from my own records. All are didactic in intent, used here to illuminate the points under consideration. For this reason they are all brief. Nowhere do I indicate the various professional affiliations of the interviewers quoted as this seems to me less important than the fact that they are all engaged in the helping interview. They are teachers, counselors, social workers, rehabilitation workers, administrators, supervisors, doctors, nurses, employment officers, as well as students in these fields. Minor changes have been introduced to ensure clarity or interviewee anonymity.

Sources referred to in the text (year of publication is noted in parentheses) are given in the Supplementary Reading List at the end of this volume, along with other books which have influenced me, either positively or negatively, and which I feel some readers may wish to consult. I have purposely omitted footnotes because I thought they might prove an obstacle to the communication I have sought between the reader and myself. In order to make up for this possible slight, in the Supplementary Reading List I have commented briefly on several of the books listed.

My views in this book are not original. I propose no new theory. Like nearly everyone else I have been and continue to be influenced by many viewpoints and personalities. We all have much to learn and always shall. Yet in fairness to my readers and to myself I wish to state that far more than anything else the work of Carl Rogers has stimulated me to try to come to grips with the helping interview. My gratitude to Dr. Rogers is profound.

I also want to say that without the active cooperation of students, colleagues, and interviewees this book could never have been written.

Finally, I want to express my heartfelt thanks to my wife Joyce (Aliza), who has patiently gone over the manuscript with me and whose editorial assistance has done much to clarify my meaning.

A. B.

CONTENTS

Chapter Three

Philosophy

Chapter Four

Recording the Interview

Chapter Five

The Question

Chapter Six

Communication

Chapter Seven

Responses and Leads

(Gradated list of interviewer's responses and leads, starting with interviewee-centered, gradually shifting to interviewer-centered, then to authoritarian, and concluding with open use of interviewer authority)

The Helping
Interview ❖

CHAPTER ONE

Conditions

Some time ago I had almost reached my home after the day's work when a stranger accosted me. He asked me if I knew the whereabouts of a certain street he was looking for. I pointed it out to him, "Straight down and to your left." Assured that I had been understood, I walked on. As I did, I noticed that the stranger was walking in the opposite direction of that I had indicated. "Sir," I said, "you are going in the wrong direction." "I know," he replied, "I am not quite ready yet."

I stood flabbergasted. Here I was. Over and over again I had tried to point out to my students that everyone possesses a life space of his own, that everyone is unique, and that we can best help others by enabling them to do what they themselves deeply wish to do. This man had asked me for direction. I had given it to the best of my ability. He had understood—I had at least made sure of that. But this had not been enough for me. Well no harm had been done. He had told me he wasn't quite ready yet, and that was that. But I was uneasy. How thin the sands on which we build! How continuously on the watch we must be in order not to help too much, not to help to the point

1

of interfering where we are neither wanted nor needed! This wasn't technically a helping interview, of course, but did that matter? We shall always be beginners, I thought to myself as I opened my front door — meaning, I suppose, that I was.

Many elements help to shape the helping interview. One must begin somewhere, and a convenient starting point is the optimal conditions we should like to create for the interview — conditions that will facilitate rather than hinder this serious, purposeful conversation we shall be embarking upon once the interviewee arrives. He is not here yet, and that is rather comforting because, truthfully, we are a bit afraid of him — not of him really, for we know nothing or very little about him, but of our interacting with him and his with us. We are just a bit anxious. As we become more and more aware of this uneasiness, we may begin to relax somewhat. Now, at least, we know how we feel. We do not know just how he feels, but we venture the guess that he feels pretty much like ourselves, if not worse.

Soon he will be here. What can we do to make this interview as helpful to him as possible? I am not suggesting that when we have more practice and interviewing has become a part of the daily routine, we shall always go through the same feeling of tenseness. I am certain, though, that both the external and internal conditions we create for the interviewee before his arrival and while he is with us are of tremendous significance. The atmosphere that will result if we succeed in our purpose will be intangible and yet will be felt by the interviewee during the interview itself, or if not then, will possibly be sensed in retrospect.

External Factors and Atmosphere

The Room

External conditions are difficult to specify since the way in which you arrange and decorate your room is a matter of taste and sometimes of necessity — of making do with what you can get. I am assuming you have a room. I once helped to set up a rehabilitation center in Israel. The buildings were far from completion, but the people in charge wanted immediate action and wired us, "Interviewing can be done in tent." We wired back, "Send tent!"

Of course, a helping interview can be carried on almost anywhere, but we usually presume that it occurs in a room. I have never been able to tell people what this room should look like. The only thing I can say is that it should not be threatening, noisy, or distracting. What belongs to the room belongs, and the interviewee will adjust to this. Under ordinary circumstances nothing that is part of the interviewer's professional equipment need be hidden away. What we do not wish the interviewee to see — files of other clients, papers of other students, electrocardiagrams of other patients, the remains of our late lunch — should be put away before the interviewee enters the room. The professional atmosphere of a room need not hinder. After all, the interviewee knows he is coming to a professional person, and this sort of room may even help him to focus on what he wishes to talk about.

Our goal is to provide the atmosphere that will prove most conducive to communication. Every interviewer will decide what this should be. The room has to be right for him, too, since he is in it most of the time. If he feels best with a cluttered desk, this will not bother most people, I suppose, unless he begins rummaging through his papers while the interviewee is talking. As to the clothes the interviewer should wear, all I can suggest is that they be appropriate. Here, too, everyone must decide what this means for him. After all, one can neither guess nor meet the expectations of all interviewees, so he may just as well fall back on his own personality and minimal professional standards.

The question of how to arrange chairs often arises. Most of the time no more than two people are involved, and usually the interviewer decides where both will sit. There is no definitive answer here either, as far as I know. Some interviewers like to sit behind a desk facing the interviewee and think that this arrangement is desirable for both parties. Others feel best when facing the interviewee without a desk between them. Still others prefer two equally comfortable chairs placed close to each other at a ninety-degree angle with a small table nearby. This arrangement works best for me. The interviewee can face me when he wishes to do so, and at other times he can look straight ahead without my getting in his way. I am equally unhampered. The table close by fulfills its normal functions and if not needed, disturbs no one.

Interruptions

External conditions that can and should be avoided include interruptions and interferences. About these I feel rather strongly. The helping interview is demanding of both partners. Of the interviewer it demands, among other things, that he concentrate as completely as possible on what is going on right there and then, thus establishing rapport and building trust. Outside interruptions only hinder here. Phone calls, knocks on the door, people who want "just a word" with you, secretaries who must have you sign this document "at once," may well destroy in seconds what you and the interviewee have tried hard to build over a considerable time span. The helping interview is not sacred, but it is personal and deserves and needs the respect we wish to show the interviewee himself. Once we appreciate this fact, we shall find a way to achieve the necessary cooperation from our associates.

Many interviewers make a practice of putting on the door a sign reading "Do Not Disturb" or something similar. Although this might be helpful, it could possibly frighten off the interviewee waiting outside or, at least, make him feel more anxious than he already is. Staff will generally cooperate if they know what is involved and are informed that you are interviewing. We need communication more than signs.

INTERNAL FACTORS AND ATMOSPHERE

It is no easier, I find, to be specific about the most desirable internal conditions of the helping interview than about the external ones. I firmly believe, however, that these are more important to the interviewee than all the external conditions put together, for the internal conditions exist in us, the interviewer.

Bringing Ourselves; Desiring to Help

The question is, What do we bring with us, inside of us, about us, that may help or hinder or not affect the interviewee one way or another? Here again I do not have the answers but want to cite two internal conditions, or factors, that I have found to be basic:

1. Bringing to the interview just as much of our own selves as we possibly can, stopping, of course, at the point at which this may hinder the interviewee or deny him the help he needs.
2. Feeling within ourselves that we wish to help him as much as possible and that there is nothing at the moment more important to us. The fact we hold this attitude will enable him in the course of the interview to sense it.

These are ideals we seldom realize entirely, but when the interviewee perceives that we are doing our best in this direction, this will be meaningful to him and prove helpful. Although he may not always be able to state it, he will probably take away from the interview, if nothing more concrete, the feeling that we may be trusted as a person and the conviction that we respect him as a person.

Trust in the interviewer by the interviewee and the conviction that the interviewer respects him are, of course, only part of the goal of the helping interview, whether it be between teacher and pupil, supervisor and worker, doctor and patient, or rehabilitation worker and client; but without these, little that is really positive will be accomplished. Our saying assuringly, "I can be trusted" and "I fully respect you" will certainly not help if the interviewee does not sense this to be true. On the other hand, if mutual trust and respect are clearly present in the interview, felt by both parties, they will not require expression in words. I think it is to the establishing of trust and respect that those who teach and write in the field of interpersonal relations primarily refer when they speak of "contact," good "rap-port" and good "relationship"; and the atmosphere that may bring these about is what we must further consider now.

This intangible atmosphere is probably determined most by the interest in what the interviewee is saying we feel and show and by the understanding of him, his feelings, and his attitudes we have and show. We communicate these, or the lack thereof, in many subtle ways that the interviewee may be more aware of than we ourselves are. Our facial expressions reveal a great deal. Our bodily gestures contribute to the picture — support-ing, denying, confirming, rejecting, or confusing. The tone of our voice is heard by the interviewee, and he decides whether it matches our words or whether they are a mask that the tone of our voice exposes, whispering, "Sham, camouflage, beware." For better or for worse, we are exposed to the interviewee; and nearly everything we do or leave undone is noted and weighed.

And so we come back to ourselves. What of ourselves do we bring to the interview? We are the only known in the equa-tion. In a way this is what the following chapters are about. But this is begging off. Beyond our assumed professional competence certain internal conditions, or attitudes, may aid us. Knowing, liking, and being comfortable with ourselves is one.

Knowing Ourselves; Trusting Our Ideas

Platitude or not, I believe the more we know about ourselves, the better we can understand, evaluate, and control our behavior and the better we can understand and appreciate the behavior of others. As we became more familiar with ourselves, we may feel less threatened by what we find. We may even get to the point that we genuinely like some of the things about us and, therefore, become more tolerant of the things we like less or do not like at all. And, then, as long as we keep on examining and wanting to find out, it is possible we shall go on changing and growing. Oriented to ourselves, we may become comfort-able with ourselves and thus be able to help others become comfortable with themselves and with us. In addition, because we are at ease with our own self, there will be less of a tendency for it to get in the way of our understanding another self during the interview.

Such an attitude will help the interviewee to trust us. He will know who we are, for we, having accepted what we are, shall feel no need to hide behind a mask. He will sense that we are not hiding, and as a consequence he will hide less. He will feel liked and may reciprocate our feeling, not knowing, perhaps, that we can really like him only because we feel positively toward ourselves. I am suggesting that our necessary presence in the interview need not be an encumbrance, that we need not be preoccupied with ourselves but can concentrate wholeheartedly on the interviewee. We can be free to listen, to attempt to understand just as much as possible, to try to find out what it is like to feel the way he does — in brief, to be genuinely interested because nothing in us gets in the way of what comes from him. We can never completely achieve this goal, but only by trying can we approach it.

Trusting our own ideas and feelings constitutes another important internal condition. Relatively comfortable with ourselves and concentrating on the interviewee, we shall find that ideas and feelings will well up in us. We ought to listen carefully to these ideas and feelings of ours as well as to those coming from the interviewee. It will always be up to us to decide if, when, and how to express these to him. I believe it to be true that once trust and respect have been established, voicing our feelings and ideas as ours and hence not binding on the interviewee may frequently help rather than hinder. I assume that such communication on our part, of course, will occur only when the interviewee cannot feel threatened by it, when he is ready to hear it and feels assured of our continued respect no matter what he does with our expressed feelings and ideas. To me this in no way entails telling him what to do. We would not do that even should he ask us to. Rather such communication helps us fulfill our role of an active, cooperating, present agent during the interview.

Being Honest; Listening and Absorbing

Another internal condition follows logically: being honest with ourselves so that we may be honest with him. If we did not hear or understand something, if, absorbed in ourselves, we could not listen to him, if we have become aware that we were not completely with him, it is far better to say so than to act as if we had been there, to pretend that he did not make himself clear or that what we missed was probably unimportant anyway. I think most interviewees feel best with interviewers whom they perceive as human beings with failings. This makes it easier for them to reveal their own fallibility.

Reciprocal honesty of this kind may at times involve telling the interviewee that we do not have the solution to his difficulty. Instead of inhibiting him, such frankness may encourage him to confront his situation more energetically. Again I am assuming that we have accepted ourselves sufficiently so that we do not feel we need appear to others as all-wise, all-knowing, near perfect. Here I am primarily concerned with integrity toward ourselves. Everyone will have to decide, of course, the point at which honesty borders on imprudence. For example, we may genuinely feel that the interviewee is arrogant or dependent, but it may not be appropriate or helpful to him to state it in that way or even to state it at all.

One last point. Beginning interviewers are often so concerned with what they will say next that they find it difficult to listen to and absorb what is going on. This is understandable but not beneficial. It takes time, perhaps, to find out that what we say is generally much less important than we think it is. When we start out, we may be so enthusiastic that our own eagerness gets in the way. We may be so unsure that we feel the need to prove how confident we are. I know of no remedy for this except patience and awareness of ourselves. The interviewee will usually set us straight — if we only let him.

Lewin (1935) and others speak of the life space each one of us occupies. What I have been trying to say comes down to this: It seems to me that when we are interviewing, it is best to act in such a way that we do not impose our life space on that of the interviewee, that we do not confuse ours with his, and that we behave in a manner which will enable him to explore his own life space because of our presence and not in spite of it. Sensing trust and respect, he may be able to launch upon this exploration in a way never attempted before — a new experience for him, then, and one he may well treasure way beyond what we say or leave unsaid.

COPING VS. DEFENSE MECHANISMS

Sigmund Freud (1955, 1936) and his daughter Anna (1946) have given us rich, new insights into defense mechanisms — things we do unconsciously to protect our ego. More recently students of human behavior have been stressing coping mechanisms, things we do consciously to meet the demands of reality (Maslow, 1954; Wright, 1960; White, 1963). Without denying the existence and vital importance of defenses, they point out that it is possible at times, for example, to cope with disappointment instead of repressing or rationalizing it away. In the type of atmosphere I have tried to describe above, it may be possible for the interviewee to cope with reality rather than defend himself against it, deny it, or distort it out of recognition.

Everyone is familiar with the old tale about a fox who wished to get at some luscious-looking grapes. When he discovered that they were too high for him to reach, he decided they were sour. Not admitting that he did not have the necessary skills or tools and instead disparaging the desirability of the grapes, the fox provides for us an example of typical defense behavior. To cope, on the other hand, is to face facts and then decide what to do about them. If we are able to create the atmosphere in which coping can be achieved, our helping interview may help more than we anticipate.

CHAPTER TWO

Stages

Well the great day has finally arrived. It may not seem so great to you at the moment, but it will soon be over and your first interview will become a part of your past. The interviewee is waiting just on the other side of your door. In spite of inclement weather he has come. You were hoping that perhaps . . . but still you are glad he is here. This is, after all, the moment for which you have been waiting. You have studied and read and practiced — all or some of these — and the time to act is at hand. As you cautiously approach the door to admit him, you feel that everything is ebbing away — all you have learned about human development, the psychology of personality, the cultural milieu; all you have practiced in role-playing or in practicums; all the things you repeatedly told yourself you would or would not do when interviewing. All this and more besides are gone now, and you feel entirely alone and unprotected with just a door between him and yourself. But, after all, it is you he has come to see; and so you let him in, learning one of the most important lessons you will ever learn about interviewing: in it there is no one but the interviewee and you. As time goes on, you become accustomed to this fact; and with a little more time you begin to accept it for what it is: the basis of the helping relationship.

You undoubtedly have interviewed before now, but you were not so conscious of it as you are at this moment — or perhaps you were not conscious of it at all. Now you are a bit frightened and uncertain. You have only yourself to rely upon — yourself and him, waiting on the other side of the door. If you could only rely on him. . . . But you can, I believe, and you will increasingly as time passes. Since he has come for a specific purpose, he may know best how you can help him. So if you can learn to rely on him, this will help you to give him the aid he requires. This important lesson may take time to learn for right now you are very much concerned with yourself and your feeling of being completely exposed and alone.

One more word before you turn the knob. I have said and will continue to say in this book many things that I sincerely hold to be true. They are true for me, and I find they usually work. But these very same things may not prove to be true for you, nor may they prove workable. The answers suggested here — to the extent that they are answers — may not be answers for you. Surely they need not be. But if they stimulate you to question them and come up with answers meaningful and workable for you, I shall feel more than rewarded for having put them on paper. The helping interview is more an art and a skill than a science, and every artist must discover his own style and the tools with which he works best. Style matures with experience, stimulation, and reflection. I am not interested in your adopting my style, but I am very much interested in stimulating you to develop and reflect upon your own.

OPENING THE FIRST INTERVIEW

I like to distinguish between two types of first interview: the one initiated by the interviewee and the one initiated by the interviewer. Let us start with the former.

When Interviewee-initiated

Someone has asked to see you. The most sensible thing to do then, it would seem, is to let him state what led him to come. Simple, but not always easy to do. Sometimes we feel we should know and should let him know that we know. So we may say, "You must want to find out how Johnny is getting along with his new teacher." This may or may not be correct. If it is, it gains us nothing except perhaps a sense of perspicacity. If it is not, the interviewee may be put in an awkward situation. He may feel that this is what he should be concerned about; and so, not wishing to contradict, he may agree even though he wanted something else entirely. The more confident interviewee will simply say, "No, I came about. . . ." But he will undoubtedly be thinking: "Why must you tell me what I'm here for? I'll tell you soon enough if you'll only let me."

At times we may be positive that we know what has led the interviewee to see us and may indicate this to him at the outset. It may turn out, of course, that we were right, and telling certain interviewees why they have come may help them to get started. However, my conviction is that if someone has asked to see us and has come, it is better to let him state in his own words just what brought him, what in particular is on his mind. Once the formalities of greeting and being seated are over, the most useful thing we can do is to help him get started if such help is necessary (it usually is not) and to listen just as hard as possible to what he has to say. If we feel we must say something, it ought to be brief and neutral, for we do not wish to get in his way: "Please tell me what you wished to see me about" or "Mm-hm . . . go ahead" or "I understand you wanted to see me" or "Please feel free to tell me what's on your mind."

I strongly object to all formulas in interviewing. Thus I am wary of such openings as "I'm glad you came in this morning," because I may not be or may not remain so for long. Nor do I like, "Please tell me in what way I can be helpful to you." I do not mean in the least to challenge the interviewer's genuine desire to assist. The point is that the interviewee does not always know at the outset what help you can give him. He may know but not be able immediately to verbalize it. He may know but hesitate to state it bluntly so soon. Then, too, we cannot be sure how much he likes the idea of having to come for help or what connotation the word "help" holds for him. Finally, our culture is so permeated with "May I help you's" whose intent is so clearly something else that it is probably best to try to help as much as possible without using the word.

Nor do I feel at ease with the word "problem." "What is the problem you would like us to discusss?" This kind of opening troubles me for several reasons. First, he may not have a problem. Second, he may not have thought of it as such till we put the word into his mouth. Third, the word "problem" is heavy, loaded, almost something to shy away from rather than to confront. I am not suggesting that people do not have problems. They may have them and not know it or not wish to face the fact that they exist. But I feel that to use the word "problem" at the very beginning, out of context and without knowing how the interviewee reacts to the word, will hinder rather than help.

And now a paradox. When someone comes to see us because he genuinely wants to and because he initiated the contact for this purpose, almost whatever we say will go unnoticed for he is anxious to get started. As long as we do not get in the way too much, he will begin to talk.

Sometimes at the outset there is room or need for small talk on the interviewer's part, something to help the interviewee get started. But we should attempt this only when we truly feel that it will be helpful. Brief statements such as the following may break the ice: "With traffic the way it is around here, you must have found it hard to get a parking place" or "It's nice to have a sunny day after all that rain, isn't it?" or "It's hard to begin, I see. Would you like a cigarette?"

Occasionally an interviewee will begin by asking: "Is it up to me to talk?" or "Are you waiting for me to begin?" or "Am I supposed to be saying something?" Here, I feel, the only possible thing to say is "Yes" or "Mm-hm" with or without a nod of the head and to add, if necessary, something to the effect that it is probably not easy but that only he, the interviewee, knows for what purpose he has come and what he wishes to discuss.

When Interviewer-initiated

The interview starts off on a different note when the interviewer is the one who has initiated it. Here I discern both a rule and a danger. The rule is simple: to state at the outset exactly what led you to ask the interviewee to come to see you. Thus the interviewer at the employment bureau may say: "I've gone over the form you filled in the other day, and I wanted you to come in so that we might talk over the types of job you're interested in and see in what way we might be of service. I see you noted down here that. . . ." The doctor may remark: "The results of those tests are in, and I asked you to come here so that we can talk about them. Now let's see. . . ." A counselor in a rehabilitation center may start by saying: "You've been here a week now, Betty. I've asked you to drop in to see me so that we can talk about your impressions of this place and anything else you may want to discuss." At this point the counselor should begin to do the very thing he said he wished to do — listen to Betty.

The great danger in these interviewer-initiated sessions is the possibility that they will turn into monologues or lectures or a combination of the two. A father remarked to a teacher who had invited him to discuss his son's problems, "If you asked me to come in just to listen to you, you might have written me a letter instead." We can avoid this danger if we are careful to stop after we have indicated the purpose of the interview and furnished the information, if any, we intended to give. The interviewee will usually have a great deal to say if he feels we are ready and willing to listen to him. If we want a conversation, good communication, we shall see to it that the interviewee has the opportunity to express himself fully. This is the only way to discover if and how he has understood us, what he thinks and how he feels. Otherwise, I suppose, a letter may indeed be preferable.

"I suppose you know why I asked you to come in" or "We both know why you are here" or "Can you guess why I asked you to stop by" are openings that if meant seriously can come across in a threatening light. Such pointless coyness has no place. The interviewee may not know and yet fear our disbelief. He may think he knows and not wish to tell. He may imagine several reasons and become confused. He may consider this a challenge and react in kind. He may then and there decide to fight rather than cooperate. It is very doubtful that this sort of opening will bring two people together. It may well force them apart or keep them apart. I believe that the interviewee is entitled to know immediately our purpose in calling him in. If it is our intention to assist him, the more honest and open we are, the more honest and open he can be. The result will be a real interview, one in which two people converse seriously and purposefully.

Explaining Our Role

Two further reflections about this initial phase. I feel it is best not to involve the interviewee in the intricacies of our role, profession, or professional background. These are of concern primarily to our employer. The interviewee may wish to know just who we are in a given agency or setup, but in that case usually he is simply asking whether he has come to the right person, whether we are the one he should be seeing rather than someone else. We need only identify ourselves and state our role in the agency in order for him to proceed with ease. If our role does come up for discussion, it will frequently be in terms of what we can or cannot do. This should be clearly explained when such a situation arises. Some examples:

"I'm Miss F., the school counselor. You can discuss with me whatever may be on your mind about Jane."

"Our agency does supply the service you are interested in. Miss Smith is the one who deals with it, and, if you like, I can arrange an appointment for you."

"I understand that we would both like a medical opinion on this. We don't have a medical department here, but we work with X hospital. Would you like me to arrange for you to be seen there?"

MAKING USE OF FORMS

Lastly, there is the matter of forms. Frankly I have little regard for them even though I appreciate the function they serve in our society. The information called for is too often reluctantly given and prejudgmentally received. As a result, forms may come between interviewer and interviewee. I think it is best, therefore, to have necessary forms filled out during and as an integral part of the interviewing process. At times this can be effected quickly and unobtrusively: "Before we proceed, Mr. Jones, there is a short form we must fill in. Should you have any reservations about any of the questions, please let me know as we come to them, and we'll try to see what's involved."

If the form is lengthy, complicated, or both, the interviewer may want to arrange a special meeting with the interviewee to work on it together, utilizing the occasion to begin establishing rapport. Generally people simply submit to answering questions as an inevitability of life unless they have been asked the same questions over and over again by different agencies or by different people in the same agency. If they then balk, one can hardly blame them. But if this is not the case and if the interviewee can perceive from our behavior that he can state his reservations — that he can, so to speak, question the question — there should be little difficulty, provided that we as well can accept forms as important or at least as one of those inevitabilities of living. A good initial relationship can be built up if both partners in the interview accept the procedure in this manner. As they work along, they may discover a lot about each other and create the proper atmosphere so that when the form is completed, the interview can flow ahead smoothly.

THE TIME FACTOR

Our culture measures much in terms of time and sets a great deal of value on time. We say: "A stitch in time saves nine," "Time waits for no one," and "Time is money." Therefore, in our culture time is an important factor in the interview. We wonder about the significance of the interviewee's coming so early or so late and of the meaning this has for him. In other words, we are conscious of time, and we assume that he is as well — and usually he is. He notices our behavior in this dimension, too. When we schedule an interview for ten in the morning, are we there and available to the interviewee at ten in the morning? This is more than merely a matter of courtesy. The longer he is kept waiting after ten, the more he will wonder whether we have forgotten him, whether he is of no importance to us, whether we are keeping him waiting for some dark purpose unknown to him, whether we are being fair with him. What this means in terms of trust and respect is obvious. Appointments should be kept on time or a good and sufficient reason provided. "I know we have an appointment at nine, Mary, but something has just come up that is entirely beyond my control, and you'll just have to excuse me for fifteen minutes or so. Terribly sorry, but this cannot wait."

On the other hand, when Shirley's mother rushes into school and insists on seeing you at once, there is usually no reason to drop everything and see her. No appointment was made, no emergency exists, and you are legitimately occupied. If she must see you that day, she will have to wait until you are free to see her. She should be told this politely but firmly. Were you to see her when preoccupied with other concerns, you would be too distracted and tense to listen to her in the way you would like. Honesty has a way of smoothing out relationships.

You should usually tell people explicitly or implicitly how much of your time is theirs. This provides an important framework for the interview. "I'm sorry, Mrs. Brown, but in ten minutes I must leave for a staff conference. Should we not finish by then, we can make another date to meet." This is preferable to continuing without saying anything but feeling increasingly pressed and wishing Mrs. Brown would get up and leave. You are no longer listening to her by this time, and perhaps you are even feeling angry with her because she hasn't finished yet and you have an important meeting (about which she, of course, knows nothing). A social worker may say: "So we have agreed, Carol, to meet every Monday at four in the afternoon until we decide to stop. We'll have about forty-five minutes each time to talk over whatever is on your mind."

When several interviews are involved, the time factor becomes part of the general atmosphere, part of the relationship. In one-time interviews this sort of time structuring is not so important, but even here boundaries must be clearly drawn. People sometimes go on talking without realizing they are repeating themselves. They may not know how to end, get up, and leave. Being products of our society, they may feel that the polite thing to do is to sit and await a signal from us that the interview is over.

I do not mean that we should rush the interviewee, but I do mean that we should make clear to him the time available so that he can orient himself within it. I have no precise answer as to how long an interview should be. My feeling is, however, that thirty to forty-five minutes should generally suffice. What is not said during that period would probably remain unsaid even if we extended the interview time, and much would be repeated. This is an upper limit; if after ten minutes both of you feel you have finished, there is no reason to sit there just because the half hour is not yet over. "Well, Mr. Kay, if there is nothing to add, I suppose we have finished. Thanks for coming in."

We shall return to this topic when discussing closing. Here I wished to stress the importance of the time factor to both interviewer and interviewee and to demonstrate that it can become a bridge on which to meet. Both should feel comfortable within the time framework; and when the need exists, the interviewer can assist by verbalizing what he sees the interviewee is feeling but is unwilling or unable to express himself:

"I have the feeling, Jim, that you'd rather we stopped right here. Am I off the mark?" or "You keep looking at the clock, and I'm just wondering whether there is something else you must attend to. We can continue with this some other time, if you like." Such sensitivity and openness on the interviewer's part will surely not diminish trust and respect but may well add to them.

A practical point: If you must interview several persons in one day, allow a few minutes between interviews to write or fill in your notes, think over what has gone on, or relax and get ready for the next person. Otherwise you may keep on talking to Interviewee A in your mind while Interviewee B is sitting there and entitled to your full attention. Get Interviewee A off your mind before seeing B. To do this you may well need a few minutes to mull things over, note on your calendar what you promised A you would look into, or just sit back or walk about to get ready for B.

THREE MAIN STAGES

Like Caesar's Gaul the interview is divided into three parts. Unlike Caesar's Gaul these divisions are not always clearly visible. Sometimes they fuse into each other to such an extent that it is difficult to tell them apart. These divisions, or stages, indicate movement in the interview. If they are absent, this may indicate that there was none, that we never got past stage one, for example. On the other hand, movement may be so swift that it is very difficult to determine just where one stage ends and the next one begins. The three stages are:

1. Initiation, or statement of the matter
2. Development, or exploration
3. Closing

Initiation, or Statement of the Matter

In the initial stage the matter about which the interviewer and interviewee are meeting is stated. This phase generally ends when both understand what is to be discussed and agree that it should be. (If they disagree, they may well part right then and there.) In actuality, the interview may not deal exclusively or even primarily with this matter. Other points may arise, and what seemed so central at first may diminish in importance and be replaced by another subject. It may develop that as the interviewee feels more at home in the interview, he will allow himself to discuss what the real matter is, thereby changing partly or entirely the focus of the interview. Thus you, the teacher, ask Dick to see you, telling him when you meet that you have noticed that he hasn't been doing his homework as assiduously as he used to. If Dick feels that you really wish to help him, that you are genuinely interested in him and not merely in his homework, he may tell you of the difficulties at home. As a result, you may find yourselves discussing primarily these difficulties and what can be done about them, returning to the almost forgotten subject of homework only when both of you, having explored the situation, see homework as part of a wider picture and plan accordingly. Here, incidentally, all three stages were covered. The matter was stated, then it was explored, and closing followed.

To illustrate further: A man ostensibly looking for a job comes to see you at the employment bureau. While the two of you are exploring possible employment opportunities, it turns out that he is actually interested in further vocational training but does not know how to go about obtaining or financing it. In closing, both of you are planning around this. The need for a job, supposedly the matter, has been replaced by something more important to the interviewee at this juncture. The real matter is further vocational training.

Mrs. A. visits her physician and complains of severe headaches. As she is encouraged to describe their manifestations — where, when, under what circumstances — Mrs. A. mentions that she thinks she may be pregnant again and. . . . The real issue has been reached, and the interview proceeds accordingly.

Development, or Exploration

Once the matter has been stated and accepted, it is then looked into, explored. Let us examine this second phase —

exploration. The main body of the interview has now been reached, and most of our time will be spent in this mutual looking into the matter — trying to examine all its aspects and reach certain conclusions. Here, just where you may feel most in need of help, I shall have to disappoint. I cannot tell you what to say or not to say, what to do or leave undone. You may wish to consult some of the many excellent casebooks available. These present case material gathered from many professions and representing various interviewing approaches. (See Supplementary Reading List at end.) This is clearly not a casebook. However, Chapter Seven, "Responses and Leads," should be of help here.

Learning from Past Interviews. Intending no disparagement of other sources, I should say that you can best help yourself by using your own interviews as guideposts — thinking about them, discussing them with colleagues and supervisors, listening to your own recorded interviews and those of others. Every interview is different. As time goes on, you will perhaps discover a pattern; but this will take shape because of the way you function, the way you are. Discovering, examining, deciding what to keep and what to change in this pattern, will provide the sort of professional and personal growth that, I feel, will be most meaningful for you.

Certain aspects of this main phase of the interview deserve careful consideration. I shall point out some of them, knowing that there are others that I can only touch upon. Again my wish is to stimulate — not to present answers but to help you find your own.

Question: Did you help the interviewee open up his perceptual field as much as possible? Was he able to look at things the way they appear to him rather than the way they seem to you or someone else? Was he free to look squarely at what he sees and to express it, or did he perceive himself through the eyes of someone else? Did he discover his own self, or did he find a self he thought he should be finding? Did your attitude prevent him from exploring his own life space or enable him to move about in it, unhampered by external influences?

When Lucy said, "I'll never get married now that I'm crippled," what did you do? You know you felt terrible; you felt that the whole world had caved in on her. But what did you say? What did you show? Did you help her to bring it out; to say it, all of it; to hear it and examine it? You almost said: "Don't be foolish. You're young and pretty and smart, and who knows, perhaps. . . ." But you didn't. You had said similar things to patients in the hospital until you learned that it closed them off. So this time you simply looked at her and weren't afraid to feel what you both felt. Then you said, "You feel right now that your whole life has been ruined by this accident." "That's just it," she retorted, crying bitterly. After awhile she continued talking. She was still crippled, but you hadn't gotten in the way of her hating it and confronting it.

When Charles, a Negro boy from Harlem, told you he hated Jews and would gladly strangle them all if he could, there was much you wanted to say. It was all on the tip of your tongue when you recalled that you were here to help him if you could. How could he realize you wanted to help him if you wouldn't even listen to him? If this was how he felt, you decided, it was better to listen and try to understand what it meant for him. And so you did not scold; you did not criticize; you did not tell him not to talk or feel that way. You did not moralize about Judeo-Christian values. Instead, you opened his perceptual field even wider by saying, "Right now you hate the Jews desperately." He poured out deep feelings of rejection, bitterness, and hopelessness. Gradually you began to see, to understand. You did not agree; you did not condone; but you began to feel what he had gone through and was still going through. You saw how full of hate and resentment he was against the Jews he knew and how totally unaware he was that you were Jewish.

Question: Did you help the interviewee move from an external to an internal frame of reference? Did you help him to come closer to himself, to explore and express what he found there rather than enmesh himself in platitudes and the evaluative labels others had been all too ready to bestow upon him?

Did you enable him to tell you how he genuinely feels, how things truly look to him?

When Michael said that he knew it was wrong to steal, did you reply, "Why do you do it then?" Or did you perhaps try to get him to sense and express what went on deep within him — his internal frame of reference — by saying something like: "You say this is wrong, but you go on doing it. I wonder what this means to you and how you understand it." You are glad you didn't probe or moralize — your internal frame of reference — by asking, "Do you have any brothers or sisters, and do they also. . . . ?" or by stating, "I'm sure that since you know this sort of thing is wrong, it won't happen any more." Interested in his internal frame of reference, you are concerned with what is central to him, not what is central to you; for the latter may be peripheral for him and in that event will shift him away from himself to you. If he says, "I hope for your sake that you don't have any sisters; they're all damned pests" and you reply, "It so happens that I have a sister, and we get along very well; your sisters may feel that the pest is you," you shift the frame of reference. But if you remark, "You and your sisters aren't exactly hitting it off right now," you do not shift but remain with his internal frame of reference.

Question: Did you let the interviewee explore what he wanted to in his own way, or did you lead him in a direction you chose for him? Did your behavior truly indicate the absence of threat? Was he afraid to express himself, and if so, what did you do to relieve this fear? Did you really want to listen to him, or did you want him to listen to you because you already had the answer to his problem, because you were anxious to "give him a piece of your mind," or because you really didn't want to hear more as you wouldn't have known what to do with it anyway?

You will have to answer such questions when evaluating yourself and your interviews. There will be different answers with different interviewees; you will not always respond in exactly the same manner.

Question: Did you go along with the interviewee, or did you force him to go along with you? Which do you prefer? What is better for him?

Iee.* When I was in the war, I had two buddies, and we used to. . . .
Ier. Well, you are back now, and I feel we must get on with your educational plans. I have the results of those tests here, and I'm sure you must be interested in them.

This sort of cutting off goes on in interviews more often than we may think. Sometimes we intend it so, and even then the procedure is debatable. At other times we don't; we just get carried away with ourselves, and later in reflecting upon it, we wish it had been otherwise. Occasionally we feel pressed for time or suspect that the interviewee is telling stories. But sometimes we are not sufficiently aware of our own behavior in not being willing to find out what is really happening.

Iee. Last night, for the first time in weeks, I slept perfectly well without taking the medicine.
Ier. That medicine is very important for you to take. Now, let's see, you are getting . . . three times a day, right?

I wonder how much we may be losing by such insensitiveness. I wonder what the patient feels about the doctor's genuine interest in him and how important this may be for restoring him to health.

Going along with the interviewee means listening and responding to what he is saying and feeling. It means enabling him to express himself fully. It means following him rather than asking him to follow us. It entails clear-cut decisions: Are we prepared to let the interviewee take the initiative and keep it as long as he needs to? Are we prepared to let him assume responsibility for himself, or do we feel we must assume it for him? Are we prepared to let him lead, or do we need to have him follow us? Ultimately, these are philosophical questions, but we answer them in one way or another every time we interview.

---

* Iee. stands for the interviewee, Ier. for the interviewer.

Frequently as we look deeply into the matter under discussion, we find that topic fuses into topic, thought elicits thought, and feeling brings forth more feeling in much the same way that stage fuses into stage in the interviewing process. However, this does not always hold true; at times the flow may falter and eventually halt. The interviewee may look at you as if to say, "Where do we go from here?" and you yourself may be wondering, too. Again I have no conclusive answer but can offer several suggestions. For one, you might express what you are feeling, "You are looking at me, I feel, as though to say, 'Where do we go from here?' " Another possibility is to ask yourself and the interviewee what is happening, "I wonder whether we have said all we are going to say today." Or you might say, "Unless there is something you'd like to add, perhaps we have talked enough about your latenesses; I wonder if there is anything else on your mind." Expressing puzzlement or incomprehension on your part, you might observe, "Frankly I don't understand what is making it difficult for you to continue." By stating this in a slightly different way you will give it a different bearing altogether: "I feel it's kind of hard for you to go on. If it will help just to sit and think things through for a bit, I don't mind at all." You have invited silence.

Many Kinds of Silence. My experience has been that most beginning interviewers find silence hard to bear. They seem to think that if it occurs, they are at fault and the lapse should be remedied at once and at any cost. They regard it as a breach of etiquette that must be corrected on the spot. In time interviewers learn to differentiate between silences, to appreciate and react to them differently.

There is, for example, the silence the interviewee may require to sort out his thoughts and feelings. Respect for this silence is more beneficial than many words from the interviewer. When ready, the interviewee will continue, usually quite soon — in a minute or so. This minute will seem quite long to us at first, but with experience we shall learn to measure time internally. Should the silence endure, we may want to interject a brief remark to help him go on; one can get lost in silence and appreciate the indication of a possible way out. For example, we might say: "There must be lots going on within; I wonder if you are ready to share some of it with me" or "I can see by the expression on your face that there's much going on behind the scenes; I'm ready to participate if you're ready to have me." Silence of this sort can be most helpful if the interviewer does not feel threatened by it or uncomfortable with it but can handle it with ease as part of an on-going process.

Occasionally a silence arises, the cause of which is quite clear to the interviewer. In fact, he, needing the respite as well, may share it. The interviewee may have related something heart-warming, tragic, shocking, or frightening, and both partners feel the need to absorb it to the depths in mutual silence. If after such a silence the interviewee still finds it difficult to continue, a comment such as, "It must have been a heartwarming experience for you," will often help him pick up the threads again.

Confusion will frequently lead to silence. A given situation may be confusing to the interviewee. He may have come out with something that confused him, or you may have inadvertently done so. Here the shorter the silence the better, lest confusion compound confusion. You will have to act to alleviate the tension in a manner appropriate to the situation and to your appraisal of it. "What I said just now about you and John seems to have confused you." This alone may be sufficient; if not, you might add, "What I meant was. . . ." and then rephrase your statement. Most likely this will elicit a response.

In an entirely different situation you may feel that the interviewee — after he or you have stated the matter to be discussed — may be confused as to what to do next. Often in this case you can help by structuring the situation a bit for him: "I see you don't know what to say or just where to begin. Here you can say whatever you like or begin where you choose. I really want to try to understand what you think and how you feel about this matter and to help you if I can."

The silence of resistance is something else again. The interviewee may be silent because he is resisting what he considers to be probing. He may see in you an authority figure to be opposed or avoided. He may not yet be ready to reveal what is really on his mind. The interviewer may well find this type of silence the hardest to deal with because he himself tends to feel rejected, opposed, and thwarted. Everyone will do what he considers best under the circumstances, but it is most important (1) to see the situation clearly for what it is and (2) not to respond as if we were being personally attacked. Showing the interviewee that we can accept this form of resistance may be an effective way of breaking his silence: "I don't mind the silence, but I feel you are resenting me in some way. I wish you would tell me about it so we can discuss it together." Or perhaps: "I don't feel that either of us is particularly comfortable with this silence. I can wait; but if there is something you're feeling, expressing it so that we can examine it together may help."

Finally, there are the brief silences, the short pauses, during which the interviewee may simply be searching for more thoughts and feelings to express. He may be thinking of how to express them or he may wish, first, to decide what he thinks and feels before continuing. This is the point at which we most often get in the way. We say something meaningful or meaningless — and destroy his train of thought. Therefore, it is best not to rush, not to interpret a short silence as a command from above to act, but to wait a bit and be prepared for what will come. Usually something will follow these short "thinking silences." Then, instead of hindering, we shall have assisted the interviewee to express an idea with which he may have struggled. We shall not have interrupted him nor made him feel that here he cannot wrestle with ideas and feelings without being pounced upon.

Inevitably both interviewee and interviewer will sometimes speak at the same moment and both then retreat with apologies and encouragements to the other to continue. This can be awkward, and a bit of humor may assist us. I am assuming, of course, that we are interested in listening to the interviewee and do not feel that we must have our say just then. We can interject a short remark: "Sorry I got in the way. Go ahead; I'll come in later." Frequently just a smile with an encouraging nod will be sufficient. Or: "I was just wondering aloud what you would say next when you said it, and now I've missed it. What were you saying?"

Personal Examples Can Hinder. During the interview the temptation to use a personal example or experience arises from time to time. In each instance it is up to you to decide whether to yield to or rise above the temptation. Not everyone agrees with me, I know, but my conviction is that for several reasons it is best not to yield. My personal experience or example holds meaning for me. I am not convinced that it will for the interviewee. Furthermore, he may well hesitate to express how he honestly feels about it lest he offend me by casting aspersions in some way on my example. In addition, in presenting my own experience I may unintentionally be threatening the interviewee. He may think to himself, "Well, perhaps that worked for you; but if I were you, I'd be sitting where you are now and not be in this mess." If he is able to express his resentment, so much the better. However, if he denies himself such freedom of expression, he may appear to accept what I have said and cause me to believe that I have helped him when I have not.

I do not mean to suggest that the experience of others may not benefit the interviewee. It may indeed. I do maintain that I hinder him when I place myself with my personal experience and example into the spotlight. However, if the interviewee solicits them, the situation is thereby changed, and I may choose to comply with his request. But even then I think it is prudent to qualify my words with a remark such as: "This has worked for me, but I can't say whether it will work for you" or "This helped me, but I wonder how you feel about it as regards yourself." In this way I indicate that it is he who is central in the situation and that he need not copy my example. He will realize that I do not look upon my experience or example as necessarily providing the solution for him.

A less confronting way is to draw upon the experiences of others by means of generalization and depersonalization. For example: "I have known many students who when faced with a similar situation have found it helpful to. . . . What's your reaction to this?" or "People do come up against obstacles like this. They often feel better when they are able to. . . . How does this strike you?" There still remains the danger that the interviewee will think he ought to adopt the course mentioned because others have and particularly because I have pointed this out, but it is only a minimal danger.

I have no mixed feelings about the following attempt at encouragement. The interviewer should avoid it like the plague. "Well, you know, everyone has to go through this sooner or later. Every cloud has its silver lining, and by tomorrow morning you'll feel much better. A good night's sleep always helps, so why don't you try that?"

Now for two more ghosts that loiter in the background of the typical interview and must be put to rest. The first is, "If I were you, I should. . . ." The interviewee's reaction: "Well, I just don't believe it. If you were me, you'd feel just as confused and unsure as I do, and so there would be two of us, neither knowing what to do. If you were me, you wouldn't say that. If you were me, you wouldn't know what to do any more than I do. But if I were you, I would never say to anyone, 'If I were you, I should. . . .'" Far better to come out with it straightforwardly: "I think your best bet at this point is to. . . ." or "I feel that right now the wisest thing you can do is. . . ." This, at least, sounds sincere.

The second ghost needs only a coup de grâce. His name is "I know just how you feel." The interviewee thinks: "I'm not taken in. How can you 'know' how I 'feel'? And if you know, so what? You don't feel the way I feel or you would never think of saying that you know." This ghost is cold and remote. If he has a mind, he surely has no heart, and so away with him.

If we genuinely feel with the interviewee what he is feeling, if we can let him know by our behavior that we are feeling with him just as hard as we can, and if we are able to show this without getting in his way, we shall not need to tell him, for he will already know. He will understand that we shall never know just exactly how and what he feels but that as another human being we are trying our best and showing him that we are trying. "I know how you feel" really says, "I don't know how you feel, and I'm not willing to go out of my way to find out."

Later on, we shall discuss leads and responses extensively. Here just a few more words before passing on to consider closing. I may have given the impression that in my opinion the interviewer should never either lead or question. What I do believe is that interviewers lead and question to such an extent that the role of the interviewee is subordinated. Naturally we must lead and question at times; but when we overdo this, we do not enable the interviewee to express himself as fully as he might. Some interviewees require leads and like to be questioned. But such individuals probably expect us to solve their problems for them rather than help them arrive at their own, more meaningful solutions. When we attempt this, no growing experience is provided the interviewee to help him meet future situations.

Closing

Stage three, closing, is in many ways similar to stage one, initiating contact, but operates in reverse. Now we must fashion an end to the contact and separate. Closing is not always easy. The beginning interviewer, especially, may not understand how to let the interviewee know that the time is about up. He may be fearful that he will make the interviewee feel that he is being pushed out. The interviewer himself may not be ready to close. Both may find it difficult to part.

Much needs to be said about this closing phase of the interview, but I have found that two factors are basic:

1. Both partners in the interview should be aware of the fact that closing is taking place and accept this fact, the interviewer in particular.
2. During the closing phase no new material should be introduced or at any rate discussed, for closing concerns that which has already taken place. If there is more new material, another interview will have to be scheduled.

It is the interviewer's responsibility to deal with these two factors as effectively as he can. The task becomes easier as he increasingly appreciates its importance and feels comfortable with it. Unless the interviewee is especially experienced or sensitive, he will not always know how much time is still at his disposal, and you can help him by indicating that closing is imminent: "Well, our time is just about up. Is there anything you'd like to add before we try to see where we have arrived?" Frequently you and he will have really finished, and you can avoid a great deal of stumbling about and awkward silence by remarking, "I have the feeling that neither of us has anything useful to add at this point." Sensing relief and agreement, you continue, "Well, then, let's see. . . ." I think most of us feel better with this sort of simple structuring. Knowing definitely now what we previously feared, anticipated, or assumed — that the interview is about to end — we can act accordingly.

There are cogent reasons for avoiding the introduction or discussion of new material at the closing stage. What happens if you do permit it? Realizing that you must shortly see someone else or keep an appointment at another place, you will not be attending as closely as you should. Before you realize it, you will be angry at the interviewee for coming up now of all times with new, important ideas he might have introduced previously. There you will sit, inwardly writhing, while he goes on talking. This state of affairs is unfair to both of you and can be avoided easily enough.

Ier. You know, Helen, I'm very glad we had this talk today. We'll have to stop now, as I've got to catch my bus.

Iee. I still haven't told you what Dad said when he came to see me last week. I didn't know he was coming, and I was in the middle of. . . .

Ier. I'm glad you want to talk about that, but if you continue now, I won't be listening very well because I'll be worried about missing the bus — who knows when the next one may come? So why don't we meet on Thursday at the same time and discuss this the way we both want to. Is Thursday all right? O.K., see you then.

You had long wondered whether Helen would ever mention her father; in fact, you had even hoped she would. Therefore, when she finally did, you were torn between the desire to hear

her out and the necessity to catch your bus. However, knowing that missing the bus would complicate the rest of the day
and suspecting that you might then feel that Helen was to
blame, you decided it was preferable to stop and arrange a
new appointment.

To close in spite of the presentation of new material at the
end of the interview is easier when both sides know that another meeting is scheduled.

IER. Our time is just about up for today, Mrs. Keen.
IEE. What about camp for Betty this summer?
IER. I didn't realize you were considering it. We won't be able to
discuss it now, but we can start from there next week, if you
like.

You do not know why Betty's mother waited until the last
moment to bring up the subject of camp. She herself may not
know. Perhaps she did so because she wasn't ready sooner,
because she was afraid to discuss it, because she hoped that
you would do it for her, because she wanted you to herself a
little longer. You could go on speculating. You might choose
to make a mental or written note of these reflections, but
you know you cannot pursue them now. Both Betty's
mother and you realize that the interview has come to a
close.

I am not suggesting that we be inflexible and work mechan-
ically, keeping one eye on the clock. I am convinced, though,
that the interview is most helpful when limited in time and
when both partners accept and work within this time structure.
Acceptance of the time factor is important, especially in a
series of interviews. It helps us to recognize that being together
is a delimited situation and that beyond it both of us are persons
with professional and private obligations that must be respected. In one-time interviews closing is more difficult to
handle. But if somewhere along the line we can ascertain
approximately how much time still remains available to both
of us and if we can begin closure early enough, allowing ample
time to pull things together, closing should prove relatively
easy.

Styles of Closing. There are many styles of closing. The style used will depend on the interview itself, the interviewee, and the interviewer. Sometimes the ordinary courtesies will suffice to bring the interview to an end. Under these circumstances a closing remark like the following will serve: "I believe that does it; we know how to get in touch with one another should anything else come up" or "Thanks for coming in. This meeting has been a fruitful one for both of us, I think." I don't mean to suggest formulas but want to stress the fact that closing statements should be short and to the point. When we have nothing else to add, the more we say, the less meaningful it becomes and the more drawn out and painful closing is.

At times in closing you may wish to refer back to the matter discussed in the interview with a concluding statement, in effect a restatement of the way you have both agreed the matter is to be dealt with. The school counselor may conclude: "I know now how you feel about Bill's college plans. When he comes in to see me, he and I will be able to take your reservations into account. You two will carry on from there, as you suggested." The doctor may say to his patient: "Now that we've decided on the operation, I'll make the necessary arrangement. Then you'll get in touch with the hospital, as we agreed." Or the placement officer at the employment bureau may conclude: "O.K., then, I'll look into the possibilities we've discussed. Unless you hear from me before then, I'll see you next Tuesday."

Occasionally a more explicit summation is required to check whether you and the interviewee have understood each other: "Before you leave, I just want to make sure I understood you correctly. You can't go back to work for awhile because of the baby. You feel that John should shift over to night school in the fall and get a job during the day. Till then his family will go on helping. If I left anything out or didn't get it quite right, just set me straight."

A somewhat different approach is to ask the interviewee to state how he has understood what has been going on in the interview: "We've had quite a chat, Jack, and I'm wondering what you are taking away from it. It hasn't been easy for you to talk, I know, and I'm not certain I understood everything you tried to express. So if you could sort of summarize things out loud, it might help both of us. If I want to add anything, I'll do so."

Sometimes in closing we may want to point up matters that were mentioned but not discussed because of lack of time: "There's the bell, and we haven't even gotten around to talking about the French or your work on the paper. We can do that next time, if you like. You know my hours; when would you like to come in again?"

Finally, when definite plans have been made during the interview, it may be well to recap them briefly during closing, especially if both interviewee and interviewer have agreed to carry out different tasks. This is a kind of mutual feedback to verify that both understand what they are to do. "Now let's see. You agreed to talk to your mother about the allowance and to try to turn off the TV by ten. I'll speak to Miss Barrett about having your seat changed. Anything to add or amend?" Similarly, mutual feedback is provided when the interviewer first states his part in the task ahead and then encourages the interviewee to state his: "I suppose that's it for today. We've made quite a lot of decisions. As I understand it, I am to look into the possibility of evening electronics courses and to check about the grant. As you see it, what are the things that you're going to look into before our next meeting?"

Closing is especially important because what occurs during this last stage is likely to determine the interviewee's impression of the interview as a whole. We must make certain that we have given him full opportunity to express himself, or, alternatively, we must set a mutually convenient time for this purpose. We should leave enough time for closing so that we are not rushed, since this might create the impression that we are evicting the interviewee. Whatever remains to be done at the end in the way of reviewing steps to be taken or summing up matters should be attended to without haste and preferably as a joint venture. With patience, practice, awareness, and reflection everyone can develop a style that satisfies him and facilitates the helping interview.

CHAPTER THREE

Philosophy

Everyone engaging in the helping interview brings along with him a philosophy in terms of which he functions. Whether he is aware of it or not, whether he can put it into words or not, this philosophy determines what he does or leaves undone and in what manner he accomplishes his task. In terms of his philosophy he determines his own role in the interview and thereby that of the interviewee to a great extent. His attitudes in the interview, which may be explicit or implicit, expressed or unexpressed, are his philosophy regarding both help and interviewing. If he is unaware of holding a philosophy or if he cannot state it, an examination of his behavior in the helping interview will reveal just what his philosophy is. Everyone deeply interested in his work will wish to discover the philosophy in terms of which he operates. Having become aware of how he behaves, he can then decide if he wants to act thus or if he would like to behave differently — to express a philosophy different from his present one.

MY OWN APPROACH

The philosophy I hold has everything to do with how I function in the helping interview and surely colors everything I have written so far and am still to write in this book. I am not endeavoring to prove that my philosophy is right or wrong, good or bad; nor can I determine its relevance for you. Nonetheless, I feel that I must attempt to state it so that you will know what it is and be stimulated to learn what your own philosophy is. In other words, I shall state mine not only because you are entitled to know it but primarily because I wish to encourage you to think more deeply about your own. Such introspection, in turn, may enable you to state your philosophy and even to change it now or in the future should you feel so inclined.

At best, the helping interview will provide the interviewee a meaningful experience leading to change. The experience is the relationship with you; change is what hopefully results from this relationship: a change in his ideas, a change in his feelings about himself and others, a change in the information he possesses about a topic important to him — a change in himself as a person. Change is possible for the interviewer as well if he can participate in the interviewing process with his entire being, but it is intended primarily for the interviewee. The latter has come so that as a result of his relationship with you in the helping interview, something about him may alter. Here two basic questions arise:

1. What sort of change do we wish to help bring about?
2. How can this best be accomplished?

TYPE OF CHANGE DESIRED

The change we want to help bring about is basically one upon which the interviewee will be able to build — one that will be meaningful to him and will permit him in the future to function more successfully as a person. The change in which we are interested involves learning. The interviewee should take away from this experience useful information — cognitive or emotional: new facts and ideas or more realistic feelings and attitudes — or all of these.

At the moment, it is clear that the interviewee needs us, and we may need being needed. Engaged as we are in professions focused on the amelioration of the human condition, we obviously need being needed and must always be aware of this need lest it intrude upon our efforts to help the interviewee not need us any longer. We must constantly ask ourselves to what extent we have a need to control his life, to tell him what to do and how to do it; to what extent we can tolerate his disagreeing with us; to what extent we can encourage him to find his own way, not ours, and become self-functioning, independent of us, as soon as possible. Helping can take place, it seems to me, in three main areas: information and resources, self-awareness and awareness of others, and personal growth.

How to Help Effect Change

I feel we can best help the interviewee to help himself through behavior which creates an atmosphere of trust, in which he feels wholly respected. We can best help him through behavior which demonstrates that we consider him responsible for himself, his actions, thoughts, and feelings, and that we believe in his capacity to use his own resources increasingly. In such an atmosphere he can confront himself and those thoughts and feelings which govern his behavior but which he hides, distorts, or denies to himself and to us. We provide information when required; but realizing that this has come from us, we wish to find out how he understands it. We offer the resources at our command and discuss their potential benefit for him, but we believe the decision as to their applicability is his to make. We act in a way that will help him become more aware of himself, his life space, his own frame of reference. We want to help him learn that change is possible but that it is up to him to decide if and when and how to change.

We behave in a way that will prove least threatening for him so that he can go on deeply exploring himself, his relation to others, and theirs to him. We genuinely feel that to learn to change in this way is good and will pave the way for more learning and more change. We do not tell him what to think or how to feel; but our behavior reveals that we value thoughts and feelings, our own and his. It indicates that the more he can discover about his own, the more he will be able to act upon them or modify them, should he so choose. We wish to help him come closer to himself and thereby to others. Being looked upon as a responsible person, he may learn to see himself as such and to enjoy applying this new learning. The interview or interviews concluded, he may continue to grow.

Playing a Vital, Active Role

I do not see the interviewer as passive in the least. On the contrary, I perceive him as active at all times. I am not implying that he should talk a great deal, but I am saying that he should make his presence and interest continuously felt. The interviewer is active in gaining as deep an understanding as possible of the interviewee's world, in encouraging him to discover what it is like and whether he feels at home in it. The interviewer is active in his interest and participation in the interviewee's searches for meaningful change. The interviewer is active in giving of himself when he feels this to be helpful and appropriate. At all times he is active in revealing himself to be a person deeply involved with another person.

The interviewer is and acts as a genuine person. He has authority from which he does not shrink, but he employs it so that the interviewee will become the authority in his own life. The interviewer uses his authority to put the interviewee in the center of the stage and to keep him there. He contributes of himself and his professional knowledge to help the interviewee, not simply to display his wisdom or his splendid personal qualities. He wields his authority in such a way that the interviewee may come to trust himself in finding his own way and his own direction. The interviewer reveals what he himself sees and understands, what he thinks the interviewee is thinking and feeling, in order to help him look deeper and try harder to reach his inner self — not in order to impose his own interpretations on the interviewee, to tell him how he should be thinking, feeling, and behaving. The interviewer puts himself entirely at the disposal of the interviewee in the latter's search for solutions, for ways to change and move forward. He creates an atmosphere in which the interviewee has genuine interest in the interviewer's awareness because he knows that the other does not wish to impose himself upon him. In his struggle the interviewee finds it important to have the interviewer react to his thoughts, feelings, and behavior.

The interviewer wants the interviewee not to become dependent on him, but to rely more and more on himself. He does not deny his authority but uses it to understand and be understood and to provide the information and resources at his disposal. On the other hand, he does not hide behind this authority to make decisions for the interviewee or to do anything the latter cannot understand or agree with. Although he acts responsibly for himself, he does not take away responsibility from the interviewee. When not sure of his ground, he admits it; and when he is sure, he knows it is *his* ground and not that of the interviewee, who needs to find his own on which to stand firmly.

"Helping the other person to help himself" is something quite in fashion today, but frequently, I fear, it is no more than a rationale to explain away whatever we as interviewers do. This goal is by now generally accepted on the cognitive level, but we all do not necessarily hold identical concepts when referring to it. Therefore, further spelling out of what I have in mind when I use these words is necessary. I mean something quite precise; and so that you may decide what you think and feel about my view, I shall be more specific. My philosophy is not new; to some it may even appear well worn. Nonetheless, I believe it is valid and operationally sound.

Coming right down to it, what do we as interviewers actually bring to the helping interview? Essentially, we bring our knowledge, experience, professional skills, the information we possess, and the resources at our command. Beyond this we bring ourselves: our desire to be of use, our liking and warm regard for our fellow human beings, our background, our prejudices and shortcomings, our own life space, and our own internal frame of reference. (All this, you will recall, I broached in Chapter One.) Optimally, this is quite a bit, and, therefore, I suppose, we succeed in helping others just often enough to keep going at it and trying harder. Now what does all this mean to the interviewee? Frankly nothing — nothing unless he perceives us and our knowledge and attitudes, unless all we are and stand for does not fall on deaf ears, blind eyes, and frozen emotions. Only as we help the interviewee to hear, see, think, and feel is he able to perceive us — after he has first perceived himself and also perhaps after he has perceived our perceiving him. I am certain that he can respond to us only after he has learned to respond to himself.

In other words, I can get through to him only if he will and can let me, if he will and can permit access to himself; only if he is able to get through to himself can he allow others to do so. The interviewer undoubtedly can aid in this process, but it will always be up to the interviewee to do or not to do, to dare or refuse to dare. We can help most, I am sure, by fully respecting the interviewee and his world and by showing him that we do so, not by our words alone but by our behavior.

Experiencing our attitude, he will become more aware of himself and eventually of us. Feeling respected, he will be able to respect what we may have to contribute. He may not accept this; but even in rejecting it, he may come closer to what will seem right for him — a decision, his decision, albeit reached through us.

An Illustration. Cognizant of the risks involved, I shall allow myself to be personal. In our culture, ironically perhaps, we hold the life of the individual to be sacred. Some time ago I received an S.O.S. to go to a hospital to "help" a young man who insisted on doing away with himself. He had recently been blinded and felt, the doctors informed me, that death was the way out. At the hospital we talked — rather, since he absolutely refused at first, I talked. I related what I had been told.

He confirmed his intention. Then I told him why I had come. My words are long forgotten, but I recall the attitude. I had been summoned to persuade him to live; however, this was not really the purpose of my coming for I felt that I possessed neither the right nor the power to do so. The decision was his to make. I had come to inform him that should he decide in favor of life, I was prepared to work with him as hard as I knew how so that life might become as meaningful and rewarding for him as possible.

This turned out to be one of those success stories we occasionally encounter. The success was his, though the respect for him and his world was mine. Had he decided differently, I hope I should have respected his decision no less; but, as is now apparent, he would have missed a great deal.

Demonstrating Respect

Respect for the interviewee and his world involves a sincere interest both in him and in it. We show this interest by the manner in which we attend him, by carefully excluding outside interference as much as possible while we are there just with him and for him, and by demonstrating that what is important to him is important to us. When we feel that we require more information or more details, we should not press immediately to obtain them if this involves cutting off or diverting the interviewee's train of expression. For if we do so, he will then think that we are more interested in what appears important to us than what is significant to him and that he must adapt his interest to ours. A thin line divides interest from curiosity. It is intangible, but I know it is there; and I think we all realize that most interviewees appreciate the former and resent the latter. They are quick to sense that when we are interested, it is for their sake and that when we prod or act curious, it is for our own.

Accepting the Interviewee

All of us have thought a great deal about the important concept acceptance and the role it plays in the helping interview. Acceptance, too, means so many different things to so many different people that I feel it necessary to explain what it means to me. Basically, to me acceptance means treating the interviewee as an equal and regarding his thoughts and feelings with sincere respect. It does not mean agreeing; it does not mean thinking or feeling the way he does; it does not mean valuing what he values. It is, rather, the attitude that the interviewee has as much right to his ideas, feelings, and values as I have to mine and that I want to do my utmost to understand his life space in terms of his ideas, feelings, and values rather than in terms of my own. Such an attitude is difficult to maintain and even more difficult to communicate to the interviewee. At times it may be misunderstood and interpreted as agreement, consent, or reassurance. And yet we have no choice but to try. Otherwise, the interviewee will suspect that we are judging him, asking him to feel and think as we do or, even worse, to think and feel as we believe he ought to be thinking and feeling.

When I accept an idea or feeling, I am telling the interviewee something to this effect: "I hear you" or "So this is how you see it." I endeavor to show him what he has shown me so that he can examine it, become aware of it, reflect upon it — do whatever he likes with it — but, basically, so that the feedback will provide him the opportunity to test whether it expresses his true self or a self he wishes to amend, reject, or modify. In other words, I try to provide the interviewee with feedback that is undistorted by my own person and personality. I return to the sender the communication he transmitted to me. The less distorted it is when it gets back to him, the more I have accepted it. There is nothing of me in this process except the way I receive his message and transmit it back to him. I am a faithful listener, observer, and reporter. What I return to the interviewee are "facts" he has stated. They may be highly emotional or intellectual; they may be clear to me or not; they may seem "good" to me or "bad" — or even incomprehensible. I report what I receive. I treat whatever he says with respect and him as of equal worth with myself.

When Bill exclaims, "My math teacher is a complete fool," I accept this, showing him his low opinion of his math teacher so that he can do with this what he will. He may repeat, modify, enlarge upon it, etc. It is probably true that I shall be able to accept Bill's statement more readily if my own opinion coincides with his and less readily if I think the reverse; but this only shows how complicated and difficult accepting really is. I may, of course, decide to go beyond acceptance. I can agree with Bill; I can disagree with him. Having accepted how he feels, I may think it necessary to tell him how I feel. I may reward or punish him, but if I wish to accept his feeling about his math teacher, all I can do is provide him with feedback and indicate by my behavior that I have understood.

When Mrs. L. tells you the apartment that was so hard for you to locate is "just an old dump," you may feel offended and wish to react accordingly. However, if you accept her and her feelings about the apartment, all you can say is something to this effect: "You don't care for the apartment, I see." This is accepting her feeling. If you resent her for feeling like this after all the trouble you have taken, you are not accepting her. I am not insisting that you should; I am only pointing out that you are not. You may even find yourself saying: "Well, I understand you don't care for this place. I've tried very hard to find you one, and this is the best I could do. I am a bit hurt, but I don't mean to criticize you for the way you feel. I do know you haven't tried as hard as I have to find you an apartment." In other words, we may be able to accept the ideas and feelings of other people but not these people themselves; and at times we may have to verbalize this.

Another aspect of acceptance is the ability to treat as a respected equal someone of another culture, race, color, or faith. Here the feedback may become distorted by our own lenses, the nature of the distortion depending upon the type of lenses we wear. Acceptance does not require strong liking, but acceptance is undoubtedly impossible when strong dislike is present. We cannot truly help a person we cannot accept, in my opinion. In such a situation the only path open to us is to deceive neither ourselves nor the interviewee but to help him find someone who can accept him. This is no disaster. On the contrary, if we have honestly tried to accept but to no avail, there may be no better alternative.

Inability to accept someone may occur even when cultural differences are absent. What is known as a clash of personalities may exist. Here, too, it is best to allow ourselves to realize what is occurring so that we may extricate the interviewee, as well as ourselves, from an uncomfortable and pointless situation. In short, in the helping interview we must be able to accept ourselves — our ideas and feelings as well — and to act accordingly. Our range of acceptance may or may not broaden with time, but we can help only when we can accept.

Understanding

The knowledge that he was understood is certainly an important aspect of that meaningful experience the interviewee will take with him from the helping interview if the relationship between him and the interviewer was positive. For the interviewee to be understood is essential to the interviewing process, but there are different ways of understanding, some of which help more than others.

Three Ways of Understanding.   Throughout the ages many great writers have shown and recently numerous psychologists have pointed out that there are three alternative ways in which one person may understand another. One way is to understand about him. I read about him, I hear others talk about him, I hear him discussed at staff conferences — I understand about him. I understand him, so to speak, through the eyes of others, not through my own nor his. This is remote understanding and is two stages removed from the person himself.

To take two simple examples: I understand about Louis that he speaks only French. And so when I meet him, I address him in his own language, and we converse. Thus I understood something about him in advance, acted accordingly, and it worked. But it is not always so simple. From a report submitted to me, I understand about Carol that she is a poor student and that she may well be retarded. When I interview her, I gradually become aware that she is hard of hearing, ashamed of it, and desperately trying to conceal it. This was not too difficult to discover. It merely involved giving up trying to understand about Carol and starting to understand Carol.

This method is less remote and one step closer to Carol herself.

The second way of understanding a person, therefore, is to understand him, not through the eyes of others, but through our own. Since this is the method by which we most frequently understand others, it deserves further scrutiny. When I understand you or fail to understand you, I use the resources at my command: my perceptual apparatus, my thinking, my feeling, my knowledge, my skills. I understand you or do not understand you in terms of myself, my life space, my internal frame of reference. If we do not speak the same language — although we may well both be speaking English — I may not understand you at all. If I am suffering from indigestion, I shall understand you differently from the way I should had the one I love just agreed to marry me. And, of course, the same goes for you in your effort to understand me, except that for you it is harder still. You came to me for help; and, therefore, in addition to everything else, you have that something on your mind about which you came to see me.

In brief, when I understand you or when I do not, it is in terms of myself, my background, my experience, my imagination. Very often, I suppose, we cannot do otherwise and at best can only be aware that this is what we are doing. Let me give a few examples to clarify: "I don't understand you. It's so hot in here, and yet you keep complaining that it's cold." This is simple and obvious. I cannot understand that you are cold when I am warm. The inference is, of course, that there must be something wrong with you. "I understand you perfectly. Had I been in your place, I should have acted just the way you did." This example is clear, too, but compare it with this: "I don't understand you. In your place I would have done just the opposite, and I assure you. . . ."

There are, perhaps, some universal human emotions, but we tend to understand only in terms of ourselves the person expressing them. I understand your expression of joy or sorrow if it is consistent with the joy and sorrow I have experienced, know about, or can imagine. Otherwise, I cannot understand you and, more likely than not, consider you "wrong" or "strange" or "absurd." I may understand Mr. A's grief over the loss of his right hand. I cannot understand the grief that Mr. B. expresses over the loss of part of his left pinky. I understand Johnny C., who likes school, but I cannot for the life of me understand Johnny D., who hates it. I can understand taking a drink once in awhile. I can even understand Mr. E., who spends part of his welfare check on drinks. But I simply cannot understand Mr. F., who spends his entire monthly check in the local barroom within a week of the day he receives it, beats his wife, and blames me for the fact he has no money!

If we do not understand another person, we may well want to find out what is causing the barrier. With time we may accept lack of communication as inevitable under certain circumstances. Then, at least, we can attempt to cope with what we are not understanding. Although the barrier will not have been removed, neither will it have been fortified.

The third way to understand another person is the most meaningful but at the same time the most difficult. It is to understand with another person, as Rogers (1961, Chapt. 17) has so well put it. This calls for putting aside everything but our common humanness and with it alone trying to understand with the other person how he thinks, feels, and sees the world about him. It means ridding ourselves of our internal frame of reference and adopting his. Here the issue is not to disagree or agree with him but to understand what it is like to be him. Seemingly quite simple though in reality difficult to achieve.

All the doctors consulted agree that Mr. Crane must undergo heart surgery. They concur it is a simple operation that is frequently performed with a high percentage of success. I may know something about heart ailments; I may have undergone surgery myself. But here is Mr. Crane steadfastly refusing to consider the operation. I want to understand with him what is going on within him, and so I shall do everything in my power to understand with Mr. Crane what this operation means to him, what lies behind his stubborn opposition. I want to share with him his strong resistance to what is, according to the doctors, a simple matter. I may not succeed, but I want to try as hard as I know how. He may eventually speak of his deep fears. If he does, the two of us can then explore them, and ultimately Mr. Crane may undergo that operation. But if I consider him stubborn or foolish or primitive, if because of his attitude I feel repulsed or rejected, if feeling pressed for time I insist he see things the way I do, I shall most probably get nowhere.

Listening: An Essential Tool. Understanding involves the use of one indispensable tool: listening. Genuine listening is hard work; there is little about it that is mechanical. Listening requires, first of all, that we not be preoccupied, for if we are, we cannot fully attend. Secondly, listening involves hearing the way things are being said, the tone used, the expressions and gestures employed. In addition, listening includes the effort to hear what is not being said, what is only hinted at, what is perhaps being held back, what lies beneath or beyond the surface. We hear with our ears, but we listen with our eyes and mind and heart and skin and guts as well.

Our goal is, I presume, to listen with understanding. This has to be learned and practiced. We must become familiar with this tool, see how it functions so that we can make it serve us as well as possible. We must understand what is involved for us in listening before we are able to listen with understanding. A simple test will show us whether we are learning to listen. It has worked for me and for some of my students as well. The test is this: If during the interview you can state in your own words what the interviewee has said and also convey to him in your own words the feelings he has expressed and he then accepts all this as emanating from him, there is an excellent chance that you have listened and understood him.

As we learn more and more to listen with understanding to others, we increasingly learn to listen with understanding to ourselves. The result is that eventually we can listen to the interviewee and ourselves at the same time without one getting in the way of the other. After all, since I am the one who is listening with understanding — trying hard to, at least — my presence is important. I act and react. As I follow the interviewee, I think and feel. Soon I shall say something; and so while attending to him, I must attend to myself as well. This can become complicated at times, for even with the best of intentions I find myself evaluating him and what goes on between us. I find myself approving here, disapproving there; agreeing or disagreeing; confirming or denying. I may express all of this, only a part of it, or nothing. But I must listen to myself as well as to him, for we both are involved, and we both are important.

There is a danger here that should be stated outright. I may listen so carefully and try so hard to understand that I become absorbed into his internal frame of reference with the result that finally I have difficulty telling us apart. If this happens, I shall not be able to help because the form of help the interviewee requires usually goes beyond listening with understanding. I must remain myself — if only to enable him to get closer to himself. While listening with understanding, I may understand something that he as yet does not; I may acquire insights into his situation that he may need to hear in order to change. If I stray too far from myself and draw too close to him, I shall not be there with my own frame of reference to help him on with his when he may most need me. I may, at long last, feel I understand with Mr. Crane what it is that deters him from the heart operation, but only by communicating this to him, by examining this with him, can I help him to take the step that will lead him to the operation and hopefully to a healthier and better life.

Suggested Goals in Listening. Beginners in the helping interview often inquire what they should seek to understand now that they really wish to listen. No all-encompassing answer, of course, exists since so many variables are involved. However, it may be important to listen with understanding to some or all of the following:

1. How the interviewee thinks and feels about himself; how he perceives himself.
2. What he thinks and feels about others in his world, especially significant others; what he thinks and feels about people in general.
3. How he perceives others relating to him; how in his eyes

others think and feel about him, especially significant others in his life.

4. How he perceives the material that he, the interviewer, or both wish to discuss; what he thinks and how he feels about what is involved.

5. What his aspirations, ambitions, and goals are.

6. What defense mechanisms he employs.

7. What coping mechanisms he uses or may be able to use.

8. What values he holds; what his philosophy of life is.

Needless to say, this is no "licensed guide"; it is merely something for us when beginning to cling to — like a hand in the dark. With a bit of light, we shall drop the hand.

Achieving Empathy

Now a little story. In one of Israel's kibbutzim, or collective settlements, there was a donkey. It was a special donkey indeed with long silky ears and large shiny eyes, and all the children loved him dearly. And so when he disappeared one day, all the children were very upset. He had been the favorite attraction of the children's farm. During the morning the children used to come in two's and three's or in entire groups with their teachers to visit the donkey. The little ones would even take short rides on his back. In the afternoon the children would drag their parents to the children's farm to see Shlomo, the donkey. But now he was missing, and the children were downcast. The sadness proved to be contagious; and before the day was out, all the kibbutz members had assembled in the large dining hall and, with concern written on all their faces, were trying to decide what to do next. They had looked everywhere, but Shlomo, the donkey, had not been found.

On this same kibbutz lived an old man, the father of one of the earliest settlers. He had become somewhat senile of late, and the children sometimes made fun of him quite openly, although the adults were a bit more circumspect. Well when the entire kibbutz population was gathered in the large new dining hall wondering what to do next, in walked the old man dragging Shlomo, the donkey, behind him. The jubilation was great, the astonishment even greater. While the children surrounded the donkey, the adults gathered about the old man. "How is it," they asked him, "that you of all people have found the donkey? What did you do?"

Well you can imagine the embarrassment of the old man and his joy, too, for never had he been paid so much attention. He scratched his bald pate, looked at the ceiling and then at the floor, smiled, and said: "It was simple. I just asked myself, 'Shlomo,' [for that was the old man's name as well] 'if you were Shlomo, the donkey, where would you go off to?' So I went there and found him and brought him back." Incidentally, Fenlason (1952) tells a similar tale. I can vouch only for my own.

This story exemplifies empathy, another important aspect of the helping interview, as I perceive it. It means feeling yourself into, or participating in, the inner world of another while remaining yourself. The old man found the donkey because he tried to feel where the donkey must have wanted to go as if in a way he were the donkey for a moment. He knew he was not, however, for he went and brought him back. Empathy in the helping interview is similar to the third way of understanding — understanding with — discussed above. The empathic interviewer tries as much as he possibly can to feel his way into the internal frame of reference of the interviewee and to see the world through the latter's eyes as if that world were his own world. The words "as if" are crucial for although the interviewer is empathic, he never loses sight of the fact that he remains his own self. Knowing all the time that he is distinct from the interviewee, he tries to feel his way about in the internal world of thought and feeling of the other in order to come as close to him as possible, to understand with him as much as possible.

The empathic interviewer explores with the interviewee the latter's internal world of thought and feeling so that the interviewee may come closer to his own world, his own self. The empathic interviewer so cares for the self of the interviewee and so wants him to learn to care that he is willing to abandon temporarily his own life space and try to think and act and feel as if the life space of the other were his very own. Being there, he may be able to understand with the interviewee; but it is only when he returns to himself, to his own life space, that he is able to help. Now he can share in the thoughts and feelings of the interviewee as if they were his own because he has understood these with him. The interviewee will have sensed this. He will have felt that the interviewer really cares about him because the interviewer has tried so hard to understand; now the interviewee will want the interviewer's reactions to what he found so that this understanding of himself will become part of the interaction.

To return for a moment to Mr. Crane, who you will remember needs an operation but refuses to consider it. After several talks, the interviewer now understands what lies at the root of this refusal. During the talks he had tried to think and feel as if he were Mr. Crane. He had felt the other's anguish at having lost a dearly beloved brother a few months previously as the result of an operation — of an entirely different sort. He had been confused as to the meaning of surgery. Was it not all equally dangerous? He had thought — as if he were Mr. Crane — of the lot of his wife and children were he to die, and had wanted to get well so that he could support them once again in the accustomed way. And right along he had let Mr. Crane know by his attitude and words that he was understanding with him. Then it was over. Mr. Crane felt understood; the interviewer reverted to his own frame of reference. He, having understood, wished to help now more than ever; and Mr. Crane, having been understood, was ready to listen. Only now could Mr. Crane hear and understand what the doctors had actually said concerning his operation. A short time afterwards it took place. Mr. Crane recovered.

Empathy is not a synonym for sympathy. Sympathy involves sharing common feelings, interests, loyalties. When related to social patterns and mores, sympathy may run the gamut from pity and charity to sincere compassion for another. Sympathy is important and necessary at times, but it is not empathy.

Nor should empathy be confused with identification. When I identify with another, I wish to be like him — to think as he does, to feel and act as he does. I wish to be like him at the expense of my own self. I wish to erase myself and to substitute the self of the other. Empathy always involves two distinctly separate selves; identification results in one. When the interviewer identifies with the interviewee, he becomes the interviewee. Thus it may happen at times that the interviewer becomes so troubled by the misfortunes of the other, so overwhelmed by the seemingly crushing problems of the other, that by the end of the interview both may be reduced to despondent ineffectiveness. Then the interviewee will need another person who can understand with him but who will remain his own self and consequently be able to give of that self in order to help the other confront his troubles and problems.

Here is a story that Coleman (1964), as well as others, relates. Many centuries ago Avicenna, the renowned Arab physician of the Middle Ages, was importuned by the friends of a sick prince in a distant land to come and effect a cure. They claimed that the prince was very ill, that many doctors had been consulted but all had failed. He, Avicenna, was their last hope. When the famous physician heard this, he became interested and asked the symptoms of the prince's ailment. The friends replied that the prince insisted on believing that he had turned into a cow and went about demanding that he be slaughtered. Avicenna agreed to travel to the bedside of the unfortunate prince.

As the prince was greatly beloved by his subjects, everything possible had been tried before this appeal to Avicenna. Treatment of every sort: pills, draughts, ointments, inhalations, cupping, bloodletting, poultices, rest, exercise, feast, and fast — all to no avail. The prince still insisted he was a cow and should, therefore, be slaughtered. A trip through the capitals of the world had not improved the prince's condition; neither had his being chained to his couch for a month. Persuasion had been tried, encouragement employed: after all, the affliction would undoubtedly pass and very soon at that; everyone knew — even the prince must know, of course — that he was no cow

but their beloved ruler. Commiserating with his dire fate
had availed no better. At last they threatened him with de-
thronement if he would not cease the disgraceful nonsense. Still
the prince stood his ground: he was a cow and must be
slaughtered.

Avicenna arrived. First he tried to understand as much as
possible about the prince by listening carefully to all — and
there were many — who wished to talk. Then he tried to
understand the prince by listening to him. Since all he would
say was "moo," this proved unfruitful. Then, as empathically
as he knew how, he tried to understand with the prince this
strange inner world of his. At last he told the prince: "Yes, I
understand now that you are a cow and that you must be
slaughtered. But you are so thin, Prince, that we must first
fatten you up a bit." Upon hearing this, the prince began to
eat — something he had hardly done of late — and to enjoy
his meals. And then slowly.... The end is obvious.

Had Avicenna identified with the prince, there would have
emerged two cows asking to be slaughtered. Had he sympa-
thized, he would have fared no better than those who preceded
him. He empathized so that eventually he might help. It is
clear that he succeeded; otherwise I should not have recounted
this tale.

We have not quite done yet with our discussion of philosophy. As a matter of fact, we have now reached what I believe
to be its central focus: ourselves in the helping interview. Let
us assume that we wish to behave in the manner proposed in
this chapter. The question will soon arise: How can we communicate all this to the interviewee? How can we let him know
that we truly respect him, that we are really interested, that we
are listening carefully to him, that we are trying to understand
him just as hard as we can, that we accept him and his world
for what they are, and that we wish to empathize as much as it
is in us to do? For we may ask ourselves what point there is
in all this unless the interviewee senses our interest and our
honest desire to help.

I cannot evade this basic line of questioning. I have an

answer. It may not satisfy; it may seem threatening or arouse a sigh of relief. Whatever the effect it may produce on you, for me, at least, it is an answer. The answer is: by our own behavior in the interview. Only this will communicate to the interviewee what we are really feeling and thinking. We are involved in this relationship as much as he is, and what we do or leave undone, what we say or leave unsaid, will get across to the interviewee. He will sense and respond to our warmth or coldness, our real involvement or our facade, our immediacy or remoteness. He will respond to us as a thinking and feeling person if we can allow ourselves to emerge as such. He will respond to anything of ourselves that we present — or to nothing of ourselves if that is what we are giving him.

The question then comes down to this: How ought the interviewer behave in the helping interview? I very much wish to present my answer because I feel it is basically correct. So strongly do I feel about this that I may perhaps sound dogmatic.

Humanness the Essence

I believe with the existentialists (Beck, 1966 [see especially the chapter by Dreyfus]; Buber, 1952; Bugental, 1965; Jourard, 1964) that the interviewer ought to behave as a human being in the interview, exposing as much of his humanness as possible. He should behave neither like a puppet nor like a technician. He should cast aside any mask, facade, or other "professional equipment" that creates barriers between the interviewee and himself. He should bring himself into the helping interview in so open a manner that the interviewee may easily find him and through him come closer to himself and to others. The interviewer should not be afraid of revealing himself. He wants the interviewee to reveal himself and hopes that the latter may learn something from him, be helped in some way. Does he wish the interviewee to learn from his behavior that he, the interviewee, must not reveal himself, that this is dangerous, undesirable, unseemly? If the interviewer is remote and cold, can the interviewee be expected to come close and be warm?

When the interviewer is cautious and wary, can the interviewee be unguarded? Will the latter be free to express openly his thoughts and feelings to someone barricaded behind a wall of professionalism? If the interviewer attempts to understand with him his thoughts and feelings, will not the interviewee want and be in need of these thoughts about his thoughts, these feelings about his feelings?

Being human in the helping interview refers to — beyond what has been said about respect, interest, listening, understanding, acceptance, and empathy — that something about our own behavior which gives substance to those very attitudes. First of all, we must be prepared to show the interviewee who we are without holding back so that he will feel encouraged to look at who he is without reservation. We must be sincere, genuine, congruent — not act so, but be so. As long as the interviewee entertains any doubts about us as human beings, he will not allow himself to trust us. He will feel that it is unwise, unsafe, and unacceptable to trust others and himself. If he senses that we are genuine in what we do and say by the way we express our thoughts and feelings, our ambivalences and uncertainties, he may learn that it is safe to expose himself through his. If he hears us and senses no contradictory message behind our words, he may learn to listen genuinely to himself without censorship.

We must learn to become ever more sensitive to what takes place in the helping interview; to listen with that "third ear" that Reik (1954) describes and let the interviewee know that we are indeed sensitive and aware, not by telling him we are, but by behaving in such a way that he sees we are. We must allow ourselves to be free and spontaneous; we must not hold back in an attempt to conform with the pattern of a "model" interviewer lest the interviewee learn to react to him rather than to us. We shall never reach perfection in interviewing, but I am firmly convinced that we can approach the humanness that constitutes its essence.

CHAPTER FOUR

Recording the Interview

NOTE-TAKING

Note-taking is an integral part of the interviewing process. We need notes to refresh our memory, to remind us to carry out our part of an agreed plan of action, to discuss the interview with professional colleagues. The most meaningful reason for keeping records may be to enable us to follow our own growth and development, to show us what we have done or left undone, how we have behaved in a given situation or with different interviewees under various circumstances. Recording can be a bridge from past to present to future performance on our part as we gain experience in interviewing.

Many Different Approaches

There are probably as many ways of recording the interview as there are interviewers. I believe it to be true that if the interviewee can relate to the interviewer, he will be able to relate to the interviewer's style of note-taking. If either the interviewer or his recording gets in the way of the helping interview, the relationship is bound to suffer. If the interviewer is comfortable with himself and his method, chances are that the interviewee will quickly learn to accept both.

In our culture, when note-taking is discriminately handled, it is not resented. On the contrary, its absence may be looked upon as negligence or lack of interest. Usually no explanation of our recording practice is required. However, should an explanation be requisite because of the needs of either or both partners in the interview, it can be easily provided. I know a teacher who when interviewing a pupil generally explains: "I won't write down anything while we are talking now because I want to pay attention to you and me. But after you leave, I'll jot down some notes so I can better remember what we talked about. If you wish to do likewise, we could even compare notes afterwards."

During the first interview with a new client a rehabilitation worker of my acquaintance says something to this effect: "I hope you won't mind my writing things in my notebook now and then while we talk. I just don't trust my memory; and if I don't jot things down, I may get uneasy and lose track of what's going on. I can listen to you best this way."

I know interviewers who feel that no explanation is necessary and behave in such a way that none is. There are those who note down straight information only. Others also record plans of action and decisions mutually arrived at. Some interviewers write down ideas and feelings expressed by the interviewee; still others note in brief their own comments as well. A friend of mine used to take copious notes. Over the years he made several attempts to cut down. During one such attempt the interviewee, whom he had seen a few times previously, perceived his effort and remarked, "You'd better write more; it'll relax you."

I have also known of instances in which the interviewee took notes and the interviewer did not. This situation may be a bit uncomfortable at first. The shoe seems to be on the wrong foot. But why, actually, should we think it is? Perhaps we still equate note-taking with being in charge.

Some "Don'ts"

Nevertheless, several "don'ts" deserve stressing. Don't turn note-taking into cross-examination: "Now let's see if I wrote down correctly what your feelings about your wife are." Don't let note-taking interfere with the flow of the interview: "Please don't talk quite so fast; I just can't keep up." If you allow yourself to become more involved with recording than with the interviewee, you are not giving him the respect he deserves and needs. Recording should always be subordinate to the interviewing process, never the reverse.

Don't hide behind or escape into note-taking: "Now let me see . . . yes, my records here indicate that at our meeting last week your attitude toward managing on the budget we agreed upon was much more cheerful." An interviewee once complained about her counselor: "He uses his notes the way my husband uses his newspaper. I can't get through to either one."

Don't be secretive about the taking of notes lest this arouse the anxiety or curiosity of the interviewee. Finally, when taking notes in the presence of the interviewee, don't write things you are not prepared to have him see. An interviewer was once called out of his office during an interview. Upon his return the man he was interviewing said, "I saw what you wrote there about me being uncooperative and aggressive!" If we consider it legitimate and necessary to note comments meant for ourselves alone and not for the interviewee — such as evaluations, assessments, conclusions — we ought not to write these in his presence. And they must, of course, be kept from him during future interviews if these occur.

In short, just as everyone develops his own style of interviewing, so everyone develops his own style of recording the interview. Both undergo changes as we gain experience and become more comfortable with ourselves and the interviewee. I have found in my own career that as time goes on, note-taking decreases in quantity, and a style conducive to good interviewing and commensurate with personal needs is acquired.

Honesty Essential

Now that we have our notes, which we took either during the interview or as soon as possible after its termination, what do we do with them? Interviewing has an ethical aspect. The helping interview is assumed to be confidential and is often openly stated to be so. This trust must be kept. Our notes, the record of the interview, are either in the form of a resume, running account, brief points that serve as reminders, or a combination of all these with possibly a summing-up and an evaluation. The tangible remains of the interview, these notes are confidential. They may be properly shared only with professional persons whose task is to help us to be as effective as possible — for example, our supervisors and those who work with us on a professional team dedicated to helping the interviewee. Although the interviewers do not always clearly state this, many of them keep certain confidential information wholly to themselves, share most information with supervisors and team members, and report only the necessary minimum to administrators. I know interviewers who keep separate files on the same interviewee for these different purposes.

Whatever the best procedure may be, I am certain of one thing: we must be honest. If the notes taken are to be used for the purpose of research, we should state this at the outset. In the event that the information gathered cannot be kept confidential, we should frankly indicate this, too. Above all, we should not promise confidentiality if we are not certain that we can provide it. The question, "If I tell you what happened, do you promise not to tell my teacher?" should not be answered positively unless the interviewer intends to keep the promise. It need not be answered positively, however, for I, the interviewer, may not be prepared to promise something about which I know nothing. I can reply: "Well, I'd rather not promise without knowing; but tell me what's on your mind, and then we'll try to figure out together what this is all about" or "I can't promise without knowing; but I do promise that if you tell me about it, I won't do anything without first letting you know what it is and discussing it with you."

Two more examples. A woman may address a probation officer in this way: "I want you to promise not to tell my boy that I came in to see you." An honest rejoinder would be, "Perhaps you'd like to tell me what you want us to talk about, and we'll see about this as we go along." And, finally, a child may say to her teacher, "You'll tell the principal anyway so why should I talk to you?" There may be no point in the teacher's promising not to tell the principal because she may be obliged to do so or may wish to discuss the matter with him. One way to express this would be, "I may want to tell the principal something, but I won't tell him anything except what we agree upon at the end of our talk."

TAPE RECORDING

In this increasingly technical age something must be said of the audio tape recorder and the more recently developed video tapes. A tape of an interview cannot be considered as merely notes. It is a complete record of what has been said and in the case of video tapes is also a record of what has taken place. Such a record can serve many good purposes, but it is not note-taking. Because of the cost and space factors involved, taped interviews cannot generally be preserved over long periods of time, and one can hardly refer to tapes as readily as to written notes. Tapes may be transcribed, of course, but this involves additional time and a specialized secretarial staff, which, more often than not, is unavailable.

The primary use of the taped interview is learning or research. Here we shall consider the former only. I know of no better device for showing the interviewer objectively how and what he is doing. The use of tapes may be threatening at first; but as one gets accustomed to them, they can be most rewarding.

"Did I really talk that much?"

"I don't recall her having said that at all. I wonder where I was."

"Boy, I sure interrupted him over and over again. I wonder if he noticed it as much as I do now."

"I was much better today. I listened well, and I think I understood what went on and expressed it. But I'm still a bit too fast on the pickup for my taste."

To me this is meaningful learning. Instead of musing, "I think I said this and that, but she misunderstood me," I can check and see. In addition, I can carry on this sort of learning by myself at my own convenience and leisure.

But how about the interviewee? How will he react to being taped? I am firmly convinced that after the first few minutes he will not react to it at all for he will no longer notice it. It is my belief that, as a matter of ethics, the fact the interview is being taped should not be concealed. If I tell him that it is my custom to record interviews to learn from them afterwards and that the tape will be kept confidential, he will usually not object. He will not be uneasy unless he feels that I am. If I can say that he, too, may listen to the tapes to learn, so much the better. If after all this the interviewee still objects, it is probably best to respect his feelings. Some people are simply afraid or suspicious. In areas or cultures in which the tape recorder is seldom used or seen, for the interviewer to insist might prove harmful indeed. When one finds he is working with suspicious people, the wise thing to do is to get at the suspiciousness and leave the tape recorder alone for the time being.

I am very impressed with the benefit interviewees can derive from listening to their own tapes. This is true for children, adolescents, and adults. At first, interest may center on the technical aspects. It may then shift to the sound of one's own voice — something we use so much and about which we know so little that often we are unable to recognize it. Later, interest usually focuses on what actually took place in the interview. The interview is a serious, purposeful conversation carried on between two people. By listening to his own interview, the interviewee often acquires a deeper appreciation of its seriousness, clarifies for himself his purpose in it, and obtains much significant insight. As far as I know, we tend to use taped interviews solely to promote our own learning. They can, I am suggesting, promote learning on the part of the interviewee as well.

CHAPTER FIVE

The Question

QUESTIONING THE QUESTION

So many regard the question as the basic tool of the interviewer that I consider it necessary to devote an entire chapter to it. Most interviewers are convinced — or, at least, they act as if they are — that their main role is to ask questions. They apparently reason that since asking questions is good, the more they ask the better. I want to question the question, that is, the use of the question. I wish to consider the various types of questions and the different purposes they may serve. If you examine random interviews, you will find most of them so studded with questions that you may begin to think the only thing the interviewer can do or feels comfortable in doing is asking questions. His questions seem to keep him afloat; take them away from him, and he will sink.

Yes, I have many reservations about the use of questions in the interview. I feel certain that we ask too many questions, many meaningless ones. We ask questions that confuse the interviewee, that interrupt him. We ask questions the interviewee cannot possibly answer. We even ask questions we don't want the answers to, and, consequently, we do not hear the answers when forthcoming.

However, my greatest objection to the use of questions as such lies deeper. It brings us back to philosophy for a moment — but sometimes one must retrace his steps a bit before going on. If we begin the helping interview by asking questions and getting answers, asking more questions and getting more answers, we are setting up a pattern from which neither we nor surely the interviewee will be able to extricate himself. By offering him no alternative we shall be teaching him that in this situation it is up to us to ask the questions and up to him to answer them. What is worse, having already become accustomed to this pattern from previous experience, he may readily adapt himself to it. Here again he will perceive himself as an object, an object who answers when asked and otherwise keeps his mouth closed — and undoubtedly his mind and heart as well. By initiating the question-answer pattern we are telling the interviewee as plainly as if we put it into words that we are the authority, the boss, and that only we know what is important and relevant for him.

Underlying this sort of behavior is an unstated assumption on the part of interviewer and interviewee which also needs to be openly stated here, namely, that the interviewee submits to this humiliating treatment only because he expects you to come up with a solution to his problem or because he feels that this is the only way you have of helping him. As for you, the interviewer, you have asked your questions and gotten your answers; now show your tricks. If you do not have the solution up your sleeve, if you cannot help after the long third degree, what right had you to ask? What are you good for? The interviewee may feel all this; but whether he does or not, you will. Having asked the questions and obtained the answers, you will feel obligated to formulate a solution, to provide "the" answer, to pronounce your "verdict." Well, if this is what you want and the interviewee is ready to put up with it, no more need be said except, perhaps, that our two philosophies fundamentally differ. I am convinced that the question-answer pattern does not create the atmosphere in which a warm, positive relationship can develop; in which the interviewee may find a valuable experience; in which he may discover more about himself, his strengths and weaknesses; in which he has an opportunity to grow.

"Shall we then," I hear you asking, "eliminate all questions?" Obviously we must pose questions at times, but — and this is a very large "but" — it seems to me that:

1. We should be aware of the fact that we are asking questions.
2. We should challenge the questions we are about to ask and weigh carefully the desirability of asking them.
3. We should examine carefully the various sorts of questions available to us and the types of questions we personally tend to use.
4. We should consider alternatives to the asking of questions.
5. We should become sensitive to the questions the interviewee is asking, whether he is asking them outright or not.

The ultimate test, of course, is this: Will the question I am about to ask be helpful to the interviewee?

OPEN VS. CLOSED QUESTIONS

Let us then delve more deeply into the matter of questions in the interview. First of all, we shall consider the open question as opposed to the closed one. The open question is broad, the closed question narrow. The open question allows the interviewee full scope; the closed question limits him to a specific answer. The open question invites him to widen his perceptual field; the closed question curtails it. The open question solicits his views, opinions, thoughts, and feelings; the closed question usually demands cold facts only. The open question may widen and deepen the contact; the closed question may circumscribe it. In short, the former may open wide the door to good rapport; the latter usually keeps it shut. It is easy enough to differentiate between broad and narrow questions. For example:

"How did you feel after the game?"
"You felt great after the game, didn't you?"

"What's the matter with you today?"
"You don't seem your usual self today. Anything happen?"

"Do you want to learn shoemaking?"
"Learning shoemaking is a possibility. Do you have any thoughts or feelings about that?"

"Where were you born? How old are you?"

"You like school, don't you?"
"Do you like school?"
"Some people like school; others don't. How about you?"

"I'm sure you love your new sister. She is adorable, isn't she?"
"Your little sister looks adorable to me, but then I'm not her brother. How do you feel about her?"

You can make up your own list and then perhaps ask yourself to which type of question you would prefer responding.

We should not proceed without mentioning the question that includes the answer. This type of question is more than a merely rhetorical one because it assumes that the answer provided by the questioner is the answer the interviewee would provide had he really been asked. It is more closed than the closed question, which at least requires an answer unknown in advance to the asker. But here there is no alternative to the answer given or suggested by the question itself.

"No one would steal unless he knew why, would he?"

"It's perfectly clear that this is how she would feel after what you said, isn't it?"

"You'd better keep away from people like that. Everyone knows what they're up to — that's obvious, isn't it?"

Similar but slightly different in implication is the question which does require an answer but which the interviewer asks so that you will agree with him, if you know what's good for you. You have no choice unless you are prepared to risk the interviewer's wrath, displeasure, punishment, or total bewilderment.

"You didn't mean to do this, did you? It was because you were upset and tired that you hit him the way you did, wasn't it?"

"You don't really want to leave us yet, do you? Just because you're angry right now, you wouldn't want to endanger your health, would you?"

"You didn't mean what you said about your father, did you? He really does love you, and you know it very well, don't you?"

"You don't really dislike all Negroes the way you said you do, do you? We are all brothers under the skin; you do believe that, don't you?"

Questions such as these may sound ludicrous, and yet they are frequently posed, unwittingly at times, even by those who find them so.

DIRECT VS. INDIRECT QUESTIONS

Next, a distinction must be made between direct and indirect questions. As indicated by their name, direct questions are straight queries, whereas indirect questions inquire without seeming to do so. All the above-cited open questions are direct. We can make them more open still by stating them indirectly. The indirect question usually has no question mark at the end, and yet it is evident that a question is being posed and an answer sought. Below are some open questions followed by indirect versions:

"It's tough working during the day and studying at night, isn't it?"
"It must be tough to work during the day and study at night."

"How does it feel to do your homework with all these little kids about?"

"I wonder how it feels to do your homework with all these little kids about."

"How does the new job seem to you?"

"I wonder how the new job seems to you."

"You've been here a week now. What do you have to say for yourself?"

"You've been here a week now. There must be a lot you want to talk about."

"What do you think of our new grading system?"

"You must have many thoughts about our new grading system."

"How do the new braces feel?"

"I'd sure like to hear about the new braces."

Perhaps you will contend that some or all of the above stated indirect questions are not questions at all. If they do not feel like questions, then so much the better. There are those who maintain that these indirect questions are questions nonetheless, and I am prepared to agree with them. I like them because they do not always seem like questions although they do show interest. They tend to leave the field wide open for the interviewee; they let him carry the ball.

DOUBLE QUESTIONS

Now we come to a kind of question that, as far as I am concerned, is never helpful in the helping interview or anywhere else for that matter. I am referring to the double question. At best, it limits the interviewee to one choice out of two; at worst, it confuses both him and the interviewer. The interviewee does not know to which of the two questions to reply, and after he has finally answered, we do not know to which question he has responded. Nevertheless, we all use double questions now and then. I do too, and every time it happens, I could kick myself. The way out, I suppose, is to accept ourselves as human beings, who must err at times, and then to make the best of the situation. For me this involves retracing my steps and untangling the two questions so that both the interviewee and I may know to which he actually responded.

First, here are a few examples of the "either-or" double question, which limits the poor interviewee to one choice out of two. He might prefer both or neither or a third; but, here he is, forced to choose from what we are pleased to offer him.

"Do you want coffee or tea?"
"Do you wish to come in tomorrow or the day after?"
"Do you want to sit near Jane or Judy?"
"Do you wish to study violin or cello?"
"Do you wish to live with your mother or father?"
"Do you want to sew or knit this morning?"
"Do you prefer to study carpentry or housepainting?"

The only excuse I can accept for this sort of question is that the interviewer has no other alternatives at his disposal or that he knows the interviewee so well that he is certain both choices are relevant. In either case, however, the excuse is flimsy. Other alternatives could perhaps be made available; possibly the interviewee has changed his mind or may want to do so. The interviewer, therefore, might say:

"All we can offer you at the moment is either carpentry or housepainting. I'm wondering if one of these appeals to you. If not, we can think further."

"You've been either sewing or knitting lately, Mrs. Smith. There are lots of other things you can do here, such as basketry, rug weaving, jewelry making, mosaics. Would you like to try something different this morning?"

As for the double question that simply confuses both partners in the interview, the less said the better. A few examples will help to show us just how confusing this technique can be and thus make us more aware of the importance of avoiding it.

IER. Did you get up on time by using the alarm clock, or did your mother wake you?
IEE. Oh . . . I just managed to catch the train.

IER. Did you watch TV again last night and leave your homework for last, or did your mother force you to sit down and study?
IEE. Mother went out to the movies last night.

IER. Are my questions helpful, and are you learning more about yourself?
IEE. I can't really say.

IER. Are you managing better with the crutches now, and how about your glasses? Do they fit?
IEE. Oh, yes.

IER. Was there an organized activity last night, and did you participate?
IEE. Some of the kids decided to go swimming.

IER. Did you study French in school, and do your folks still speak it at home?
IEE. I have a cousin living in France. She took up English in school and invited me to spend the summer with her.

IER. How's your Dad coming along, and how is Mother's job?
IEE. My brother Jack is home on leave right now. He told me that there's a new ruling and I may be able to enlist in the fall.

Perhaps I have belabored the point; but since we can never obtain a single, meaningful reply that answers two questions, it is best to ask them separately, that is, if they need to be asked at all. Otherwise, the interviewee may give up and answer neither, thereby taking things into his own hands — as we can see he has done in the examples above.

BOMBARDING

Before passing on to another aspect of the question, I cannot resist pursuing the frequent absurdities of the double question to an even greater absurdity. I am referring to what is known as "bombarding" with questions. Here the tool becomes a weapon wielded against the interviewee, if not in a deadly manner, at least in one that can hardly inspire trust, make for rapport, or create an atmosphere in which the partners in the interview can mutually examine the matter at hand. Instead, the interviewee finds himself caught in a hailstorm of questions; and if he runs to the nearest shelter, we can only admire his urge to survive. I shall give one example without further comment as it speaks for itself. "Well, why don't you answer? Do you need more time to think? Isn't there anything you can say? Didn't I make myself clear enough? Do you think that I don't know what has been going on or that I don't care? Would you rather I stop asking? Would you rather I leave you alone for awhile?" Until she heard her own tape, this interviewer claimed that she had tried to get the interviewee to talk and that he had refused.

I seem to hear someone raising the objection that this example is too extreme and that I am being facetious. Be this as it may, bombarding and probing are no less present in the following excerpt, though not so obvious at first glance or at first hearing:

IER. Hello, Jack, come right in. I'm the placement officer at the center. I understand you'll be leaving us soon. What would you like to do when you get out?

IEE. I don't exactly know. You see. . . .

IER. What have you done in the past?

IEE. Well, I tried my hand at several things, but then I got sick and. . . .

IER. Yes, I know. Did you ever learn a trade or go to trade school?

IEE. I started welding but. . . .

IER. Right. That's out now. Is there something you're interested in now?

IEE. I was thinking that perhaps merchandising. . . .

IER. What did the vocational counselor suggest? Did he discuss your test results with you?

IEE. He thought merchandising might be all right, but he said I'd need more education than I've had.

IER. How much have you had?

IEE. Eight years.

IER. How old are you now?

IEE. Going on twenty.

IER. Are both of your parents alive? Will you be staying with them when you leave us?

IEE. I sure hope so because . . . at first . . . I'll need help . . . and. . . .

IER. Do you think you'd like to go back to school for awhile?

IEE. I suppose so, but I don't know whether financially. . . .

IER. Just what is your financial situation at the moment?

IEE. Well, it isn't very good.

IER. What appeals to you about merchandising?

IEE. Contact with people and goods, I suppose.

IER. Did you have anything else in mind?

IEE. I like the law.

IER. Were you thinking of becoming a lawyer?

IEE. I don't know. I think Dad would like me to help him around the farm if I could . . . I mean, if the doctors agree.

IER. What kind of farm does your Dad have?

IEE. Practically everything but no cows.

IER. Anything else besides merchandising and the law interest you?

IEE. Well, I used to do some photography.

IER. That sounds interesting. What did you used to do?

This, I think, is probing with the best of intentions. The interviewer means to help, and the interviewee seems ready for and in need of help. But so much bombarding is going on that neither can really help the other. They can hardly keep up with what is being said, let alone explore Jack's thoughts and feelings. No attempt is made to enable him to express himself fully. No wonder he should feel it is up to the interviewer to find the solution. Nothing has been done to encourage him to arrive at one or to make him feel that he may be capable of doing so. Unhappily, this example is not extreme. I wish it were.

THE SHOE ON THE OTHER FOOT

Now let us put the shoe on the other foot. What shall I do with the questions the interviewee addresses to me? What if he probes or bombards me with questions? I have no comprehensive answer to this, but there is, I believe, a helpful approach, which I wish to share with you.

I feel certain that we ought not to reply to every question. At times ethics may even prevent us because by so doing we might betray the confidence of someone else. On the other hand, we should, I feel, respond to every question we are asked and treat each question just as we do everything the interviewee says — by listening to it with as much understanding as possible and being as helpful as we can in our response. Not every question calls for an answer, but every question demands respectful listening and usually a personal reaction on our part.

It is interesting to note in passing that although interviewers are quite prepared to use questions freely — very often too freely — they are unprepared for and more or less wary of questions directed at them. Perhaps these are the two sides of the same coin. If we can learn to threaten less with our questions and to feel less threatened by questions directed at us, we shall be better practitioners of the helping interview. Once we see the question as one of the ways in which the interviewee expresses himself, we may not be perturbed by his asking. We may not be jolted into a defensive attitude based on the reasoning, "I must have done something wrong if he's beginning to cross-examine me." This attitude will almost inevitably communicate itself to the interviewee: "I'm supposed to ask the questions around here. Who do you think you are, questioning me?"

Examining our "danger" a bit closer, I think that the interviewee may conceivably question us about three areas of interest to him: others, ourselves, and himself. (I am not taking into account rhetorical questions, to which no one really expects an answer. We must simply learn to identify these and remain silent.)

There is a fourth area — that of seeking information — but it is more apparent than real. Usually it is a cover for or extension of one of the three above-mentioned areas; and should we fail to understand this, we may miss a great deal of the ongoing interaction. I am not suggesting that questions which obviously request information should not be treated at face value. I am suggesting that we be careful and always verify that there is nothing hidden beneath the surface which warrants a response as well. "What time is it?" sounds innocent enough. However, in the interview it may mean: "How much longer must I take this?" or "I wish this would go on, but I know it won't" or "I hope you won't keep me much longer; I'm missing all of my gym period." If feelings such as these are hidden behind the questions, our providing information alone would indicate that we are not sufficiently sensitive to what is taking place. A sensitive response to the feelings behind the question might be: "I wonder what your feelings are about our talk this morning" or "Time seems to fly today, but we'll have to stop soon" or "Are you wondering how much longer I shall be keeping you? What subject are you missing now?"

Thus we ought to supply the information requested when it is feasible and appropriate to do so, but we should always be open to the possibility that there is something behind and beyond the question which is worth getting at. I am not speaking of probing such as that in the following example (it is no secret by now what I think of probing): "It's nine thirty-five. I've told you the time; now why don't you tell me what you really wanted to ask. Come on, don't be afraid; I won't bite."

Particularly with these straightforward requests for information we must keep our "third ear" working; for although ostensibly asking a question, the interviewee may be communicating something else. I recall that once I was asked my name early in an interview. I supplied it, thinking the interviewee might well have known what it was. I added this and wondered aloud whether he had any feelings about the name. He had — very strong ones — and the interview was on its way. I do not mean to make a mountain of a molehill. Nothing may be concealed behind the interviewee's question, but it is worth while to examine it sensitively just in case there is.

When the interviewee questions us more specifically in any of the three areas mentioned, I believe the approach should be the same: to respond at all times in a manner helpful to the interviewee; and to be sensitive and honest when we answer the question and also on those occasions when we do not answer it. If we can relate our response back to the interviewee, we shall generally not go wrong.

Interviewee's Questions About Others

Let us consider now the interviewee's questions about others. For example: "The woman who left just as I came in seemed quite upset. Did you give her a hard time?" What shall we do with this? Surely not ignore it and just as surely not answer it directly. After all, her interview was confidential just as his is now. Perhaps he is concerned about himself and the hard time he fears I may give him. Therefore I might honestly respond, "I can't tell you about her, of course, just as I couldn't tell her about you; but I'm wondering whether you're uneasy about our meeting, feeling I might give you a hard time?" An alternative way would be to ignore entirely the reference to the woman, as if it were understood that she would not be discussed, and to say, "I suppose you're wondering how you and I are going to get along."

Many possibilities exist in this area in which the interviewee questions us about others. I wish to touch briefly upon only these: (a) when the other person has been known to both the interviewer and interviewee prior to their present contact; (b) when the person is known to the interviewee only; (c) when as a result of the helping relationship the interviewer meets the other person, known previously to the interviewee only.

In the first instance the interviewee may say to us: "Well, now I've told you the way that doctor treated me. What do you think of him?" We may wish to express our opinion of him. Whether we do or not, it is usually best to revert to the interviewee's frame of reference. "I personally like him very much, but I understand you feel he has treated you pretty coldly, sort of like a number instead of a person."

When the other is unknown to us, it is all the easier to shift back to the interviewee's life space: "I don't know Dr. L., but I get the feeling that you like him so much you are just a bit sorry he helped you to get well so fast and brought you to the point that you are ready to leave the hospital the day after tomorrow."

When the interviewee knows we have become acquainted with the other person (who may be close to him), a situation can arise that interviewers will handle in different ways. The interviewee may say: "So now you've met my mother. She must have told you plenty about me. What did she say? Come on, don't pretend she didn't." Although the following interviewer responses are dissimilar, they have three things in common: the interviewer is honest about what he reveals or does not reveal, he expresses his thoughts and feelings sincerely when doing so at all, and he ends up by reverting to the life space of the interviewee.

"You know, June, I can't tell you what she said, just as I couldn't tell her what we've been talking about. We had a good long talk, and as a consequence I think I better understand your relationship with your mother and hers with you."

"Your mother asked me not to discuss our talk with you. She'd rather you ask her directly what she said to me. I wonder how you feel about that."

"Your mother did say things about you that you may consider 'bad' of her to think or feel. I got the impression that she really thinks and feels as she says. She just sees things differently from the way you do. For example, she really feels you stay out too late at night and that as a result your studies suffer. She very much wants us to discuss this further. Have you done any more thinking about what we said last week?"

Interviewee's Questions About Us

The second area is the one in which the interviewee directly questions us about ourselves. Here again I can suggest only an approach. Answer directly when appropriate, do not take over the stage for long, and revert to him as soon as possible.

IEE. You're a wonderful person to be able to listen to me the way you do. Isn't it hard on your nerves though?

IER. I'm glad you like me, Hank. I was getting a bit nervous, and I'm glad you brought it up. You've been smoking one cigarette after the other this evening. I think I just got nervous watching you being nervous. There's something you want to talk about but haven't been able to yet, isn't there?

IEE. You've got on a different dress again today. How many dresses do you own?

IER. Not all that many, really; I just alternate a lot. You pay lots of attention to my clothes. How does it feel to wear the uniforms you have to wear around here?

IEE. Do you have any children of your own?

IER. Yes I do, two boys. The elder one is Jimmy's age. I wonder if you got around to talking to Jimmy's teacher about the lunches.

IEE. Have you ever been divorced?

IER. No I haven't. Are you perhaps saying that no one who hasn't been through what you have will be able to understand?

IEE. How do you feel about being blind?

IER. Well, can't say that I like it. I think I'm trying to do what you are, which is to manage as well as possible. I've been at it longer, though, and so it may be easier. You know, you've never really spoken of your feelings about blindness or about anything else, for that matter, since we started our talks. I wonder if the ice is beginning to melt some.

Interviewee's Questions About Himself

The last area consists of questions that the interviewee poses about himself. Without repeating what has already been said, I shall cite some examples that reflect the same approach:

IEE. Should I major in French or Spanish?

IER. That's what we want to decide together. So far, I know that you could master either, that you like both, but that. . . .

IEE. Do I look sick to you today?

IER. Do you feel sick today?

IEE. Have you made up your mind yet as to the "type" I am?

IER. Frankly my mind doesn't run along those lines. I don't see you as a "type." I'm trying to see you as you, as Paul. I think you may need to classify people and so perhaps think I do.

IEE. Do you think I should take that job?

IER. I see that it is very hard for you to decide. I can't tell you whether you should take it or not, but I can try to summarize the pros and cons as I understand them from your point of view. Well. . . . Now I'll add some that I have been thinking about. . . . It's not an easy decision to make, and I want to help you as much as I can to make up your own mind one way or the other.

IEE. Look at me! Would any boy ever want to get close to something like me?

IER. I think you're asking me if you will ever have a boyfriend or perhaps if any man will ever want to marry you. Honestly I don't know. At first I found it hard to look at you, but I don't any more. I don't know, either, what can still be done in a medical way. But you know, Judy, I find it much easier these days to look at you than to listen to you. I'm not criticizing, only telling you how I feel. You sound hard — you sound so hard I get the feeling that if any boy were to try to get near you, you would push him away just to prove to yourself that no one wants to get close.

I have a slight suspicion that this section somewhat resembles a cookbook, though all I meant to do was to suggest possible ways of approaching the stove without getting burned. How to respond to the interviewee's questions, when and if to reply, are such personal matters for the individual interviewer and depend so much on the individual interviewee that I am not certain I have succeeded in what I set out to do — to offer an approach that I find helpful. I trust you will find your own whatever you may decide to do with the above.

"WHY"

The single word that symbolizes inquiry more than any other and is most frequently employed in asking questions is the little word "why." At the outset of this discussion I want to confess that I have an aversion to the way the word is generally used, if not to the word itself. A legitimate basis for the use of this word in our language undoubtedly exists, but I maintain that "why" has so often been misused its original meaning has become distorted. It was once a word employed in the search for information. It signified the investigation of cause or reason. When employed in this manner even today, it is appropriate, and I know of no other to take its place. Unfortunately, this is generally not the way it is used at present.

Today the word "why" connotes disapproval, displeasure. Thus when used by the interviewer, it communicates that the interviewee has done "wrong" or has behaved "badly." Even when that is not the meaning intended by the interviewer, that is how the word will be understood. The effect upon the interviewee will be predictably negative, for he will most probably have grown up in an environment in which "why" implied blame and condemnation. Naturally enough, he will react to the word in the interview the way he has learned to react to it over the years even though the interviewer may have used it simply in the sense of genuine inquiry. Thus whenever the interviewee hears the word "why," he may feel the need to defend himself, to withdraw and avoid the situation, or to attack.

In their early years children use the word frequently — often to our distraction. For them it is a key to unlock the secrets of the world about them; it enables them to explore and discover. They ask for information without implying moral judgment, approval or disapproval. But they learn. They learn that the adults surrounding them use the word differently — to put them on the spot, to show them they are behaving in an unacceptable manner. Slowly but surely the children stop using the word for the purpose of inquiry and begin to employ it against others the way it has been used against them. The child's ears ring with the questions: "Why did you muddy my clean floor?" "Why are you barefoot?" "Why don't you use your knife and fork properly?" "Why did you break that dish?" etc., etc. He learns to imitate his elders. Soon enough he will say to his friend, "Why did you take my bike?" to show that he disapproves of the act and not because he is interested in obtaining a bit of useful information. He will say to his mother, "Why must I go to the store?" not because he wants a reason but because he doesn't wish to go. This is his way of saying, "No, I am against it."

At the same time children discover a way to defend themselves against the threatening word. In countries where English is spoken they will answer "because" when asked "why." In Israel the word for "why" is "lama," and the answer the children supply is "kova." This means literally "hat" and is as senseless, of course, as they perceive the question itself to be. Such replies are more than a defensive maneuver, however. They indicate that the children are learning to play the game according to adult rules. They have discovered that there is no meaningful reply to the question and that none is, in fact, anticipated. Whenever they hear the word "why," they now know that what is really meant is, "Change your behavior; act the way the adults, the strong ones, want you to act." And they respond accordingly.

Later on they learn an additional lesson. Day in and day out in school they hear: "Why are you late?" "Why didn't you do your homework?" "Why can't you listen?" "Why don't you answer?" When they attempt a reply, either they are not listened to or, even worse, they are punished twice over. So they learn not to reply at all. They may or may not change their behavior; they may submit or revolt; they may succeed or fail in adapting themselves to their adult environment. Whatever the outcome, the little word "why" has become anathema.

This is the main reason for my strong aversion to the use of "why" in the helping interview. Regardless of the interviewer's intended meaning, "why" is too often perceived as "Don't do that" or "I consider this bad" or "You ought to be ashamed." Consequently, the interviewee will withdraw into himself, attack, or rationalize, but he will not come closer to us or to himself. He will not feel free to explore and examine but feeling threatened, will need to defend himself as best he can. Here are some examples:

IER. Why did you talk to Bill in class today?

IEE. I didn't . . . I didn't talk to Bill.

IER. But I saw you talking to him during math class.

IEE. Oh, that was nothing. I won't do it any more. I just asked him. . . .

IER. But, Charlie, I don't mean to scold you. I just wanted to know why. You know, you boys have been ignoring him ever since he came into our class, and I was glad to see that at last. . . .

The intentions were good, and the harm done was probably not great. But it could have been avoided so easily had the teacher told Charlie at the outset that she had noticed him talking to Bill and wished to find out from him what was going on between them, whether there was really a change.

IER. Mary, could you tell me why your mother came to see you last night?

IEE. I'm sorry, Miss Jones. I know parents aren't supposed to stay after nine, but . . . it was important . . . it won't happen again.

IER. But, Mary, I wasn't finding fault. I didn't even know she was here after nine. I noticed that both of you looked quite concerned and. . . .

Again no real harm was done, but this misunderstanding as well could easily have been avoided. Both Charlie's teacher and Miss Jones were honest and interested and not out to find fault. However, they were perceived in another light by the interviewees, who assumed from past experience that the way they were being questioned meant they had done wrong. Only after this misconception had been rectified could both interviews progress in a manner helpful to all concerned. In interviewing the less clearing up we have to do the better, because trust and respect do not stand up well under the strain.

Unfortunately, I cannot yet rest my case. Even assuming that the negative connotations associated with the word "why" have been exaggerated here or that they can be rectified by the interviewer, I should still object to the misuse of the word. More often than not, interviewees perceive it as probing, and all too frequently interviewers resort to it to express their frustration with the interviewee, themselves, or both. The "why" seems to demand of the interviewee an answer that he may not possess, one that is unclear to him, or one that he is not willing to share — at least not yet, perhaps because of the way the interviewer is going about obtaining it. Often a tug-of-war will result to test who can hold out longer. Whatever the outcome may prove to be, in my opinion it does not justify the method.

I may sincerely want to know the why of someone's behavior: the cause, the reason, the need, the motivation, the explanation. And so I ask, "Why?" It is easier for me to ask than for the interviewee to reply. For one thing, he may not really know why; he himself may be puzzled by his conduct. Or he may be groping for the answer and finding several possibilities. Different, even contradictory, forces may be impelling him or holding him back. He may even know or, at least, think he knows but not wish to reveal it. He may be confused, ashamed, or even amused — he may simply decide to keep this "self" secret to himself. Whatever the reason, this kind of probing and pushing is distinctly unhelpful. We may extract an answer of sorts, but, more likely than not, it will be one produced to satisfy us, one the interviewee feels we want to hear, rather than a true, significant step forward for him in his understanding of himself.

Often we shall have our answer but at too high a price. We may cause the interviewee to close rather than open up, defend rather than look within, rationalize rather than cope with his own truth. A few common examples will illustrate what I have in mind:

IER. Why were you late again this morning Jean?
IEE. The bus didn't stop again. Too crowded.

This answer may or may not satisfy the teacher, but Jean knows there is more to it than that. She can't, she won't, put it into words. Another quarrel at home this morning — screaming and crying — and it didn't seem worth while getting up. It was safer under the covers, pretending she was still asleep. But she won't tell her teacher that; she will hardly admit it to herself. The crowded bus story sounds as good as any other.

Let the teacher do with it what she will. Jean might have
allowed herself to be more honest with herself and the teacher
had the interview begun differently, had the teacher said something like this: "I've noticed, Jean, that you've been coming in
late these past few days. I wonder if there's something wrong
and if we here at the school can help. I can stay after class
today. Perhaps we can get together then and talk about it.
What do you think?"

Here are some other examples:

"Now, why didn't you take that job, Joe? We agreed you
would. Other people would have jumped at the chance. Why
didn't you go out there? There aren't that many jobs around,
you know, and I was sure you would try it. You said you
would. Why didn't you?" The interviewee remained speech-
less. He himself didn't know why. Mr. Gates was right, but
he couldn't tell him so. He couldn't tell himself. It had something to do with that hand. He thought he was over that. He
knew Mr. Gates thought he was over that. He had taken the
subway out to the place. He had repeatedly told himself that
this time he would see it through. And, then, he had felt that
hand in his pocket — or rather the lack of it — and before he
knew where he was, he was back home again. He remained
silent, confused, ashamed. Only much later did he understand
all this; only much later could he feel how he had felt and
verbalize it. Right now he hated himself and Mr. Gates, who
became increasingly impatient. Joe finally produced an answer,
"I couldn't find the place." Mr. Gates retorted: "You couldn't
find the place . . . after all the explanations! Well, something
else turned up today. It's right in your neighborhood. I'm sure
you can do the work. Want to try it?" Mr. Gates had calmed
down. He had received his answer.

"Why didn't you take those pills I prescribed? Didn't I tell
you how important it is for you to take them?" Mrs. Bell tried
hard not to cry. She knew the doctor meant well. She also
knew how busy he was and how long it would take her, her of
all people, if she tried to tell him why. She knew exactly why,

too. She didn't know if she was right or not, but she didn't care about that. She knew she didn't care if she got well again. As a matter of fact, she got more attention being sick than being healthy. She knew lots of things — about her kids and their kids and the way they had gotten her into that home. And about the home . . . she knew plenty about that, too. But the doctor wanted to know why she hadn't been taking those pills, and so she thought fast, "I'll take them from now on, Doctor; you'll see." The doctor was pleased. He smiled, held out his hand, and ushered her out of the office. He really didn't want to know why. He just wanted her to take the medicine. He liked the old lady but was too busy to waste time.

"Why did you do so badly on those college entrance exams, a bright fellow like you?" Jack replied, "I really don't know; I can't figure it out." The counselor prodded: "But you must know; you must have some idea, at least. After all, you took them, not I. Why did you do so poorly?" Jack really didn't know — at least he wasn't aware of the fact that perhaps he did. He felt the counselor was annoyed with him and seemed to care more about why he had done so badly than about the fact that he had. Not knowing what to say, he said nothing.

I hope I have made my point. All the interviewees cited above felt threatened, prodded, pushed. They did not feel that the interviewer cared about them, respected them, really wanted to help them. They were not enabled to express what they thought and felt. They perceived themselves as rejected, misunderstood, imposed upon. Hence they withdrew, prevaricated, or hit back even if the only weapon with which they could hit back was silence.

Should the word "why," then, never be used? I know I wish I myself would employ it less, for in spite of all my reservations and objections to its use, it keeps on cropping up. I try to avoid it and am glad when I succeed, but often enough there it is to be dealt with again. The little word, however, does have a justifiable place, and this is the one additional point I want to make here. If the interviewee perceives that our attitude is unthreatening and if we use "why" simply to obtain factual information that the interviewee possesses and we feel we need, then our use of the word should not cause undue damage. Perhaps I am saying this to comfort and solace us as we continue asking "why," but I hope this point is indeed legitimate.

For all the reasons given above, I feel that we should use "why" as sparingly as possible and that when we do use it, we should do so to get at facts rather than feelings, at thoughts rather than emotions. In our culture facts and thoughts are more readily accessible, more easily disclosed, than feelings and emotions. In a nonthreatening atmosphere in which trust and respect are present, I think one might inquire:

"Why did you move to our city?"

"Why do you wish to register your child at this school?"

"Why are you planning to come back to work after all those years you spent at home?"

If, in spite of our precautions, we sense that our question has placed the interviewee in an awkward position, we can still retreat and rephrase it. As careful as we may be, we never know for certain how someone else will perceive a question that we regard as entirely innocuous and factual. We can only be as sensitive as we are and strive to become as sensitive as it is within us to become.

CONCLUDING REFLECTIONS

H. S. Sullivan, the noted American psychiatrist who, incidentally, wrote an entire book on the psychiatric interview (1954), knew how to listen to his patients. He would listen with great concentration, trying to understand. Then suddenly he might come out with something like this: "Well isn't that interesting?" as if to imply: "So what? Where do we go from here?" A comment like this is what I seem to be hearing now as I approach the end of the chapter. I did not intend to kill the question in this long tirade. It has its place in the helping interview — such an important place indeed that I had no choice but to go into the matter at length. The question is a useful tool when used delicately and sparingly. Too often, I fear, it is employed like a hammer. When used indiscriminately, it hampers progress. When used threateningly, it is dangerous. I do not retract a word of what I have written, but I feel I cannot be let off so lightly. The issue still remains: How and when can the question be used to advantage in the helping interview? I think I have answered this implicitly in the preceding pages, but to round off the discussion I shall now be explicit.

How to Use Questions

Let's consider the how. Except when our questions are for the purpose of filling out forms or obtaining needed specific information (when the closed question may prove unavoidable) they ought to be, I am convinced, as wide open as possible. They should be single questions, not double or multiple ones. They should be stated as succinctly as possible and still remain clear and understandable. If they can be indirect rather than direct, so much the better. The fewer direct questions we ask, the more likely it is that we shall not create an atmosphere of "I'm here to ask the questions, and you're here to answer them." I strongly favor eliminating the "why" questions as much as possible. One final point. After we have asked the question, we ought to stop right there and wait for and listen to the answer. If we do not, this ought to tell us something about the questions we are asking. We may discover that they are not nearly as important and meaningful as we may have believed. Listening with understanding to our own tapes can be most revealing in this respect.

When to Use Questions

Next the when. One situation that calls for questions is that in which we have been unable to hear, listen, or understand for one reason or another. I think it is better and more honest to inquire rather than to substitute for missed words those we surmise were spoken. We may go about this without asking a question directly, but the effect will be the same:

"I'm sorry. I missed that last part. What did you say?"

"I didn't catch your question about Joe. I was too engrossed in noting how nervous you seem."

"It's too bad about this interruption, but I just couldn't prevent it. Where were we when I was called out?"

Such questions may reveal some of our shortcomings but will not, I believe, push the interviewee away. In showing him our concern, our interest, our human fallibility, they may well bring him closer.

A second situation relates to whether we have been understood by the interviewee. At times we talk more than we intend or express ourselves clumsily; then we wonder whether we have gotten our intent across. Occasionally we may say little, and the little we say seems to us unambiguous; yet we wonder whether we have been understood correctly. Sometimes we simply feel the need for feedback from the interviewee to be certain that he has perceived us as we meant to be perceived. Whatever the case, I feel it is preferable for us to voice our doubts rather than to remain silent and keep wondering. Otherwise, the uncertainty may increase and blemish the relationship that has been built up.

"I'm afraid I've been rambling on. What did you understand me to say?"

"I haven't made this very clear, have I? What sense, if any, did it make to you?"

"Well, that's it. I felt you really wanted my honest view on this matter. Now I should very much like your honest view of mine. What do you think of it all?"

"I have the feeling we've been talking at cross purposes for the past few minutes. I think it would be helpful to hear more from you about your suggestion so that we may understand each other better."

Third, I may want to phrase a question to assist the interviewee in clarifying or exploring further a thought or feeling he has been expressing. It may be just to let him know that I am with him, listening and trying to understand; or sensing that a little structuring may help him carry on, I may phrase a question to provide this. My intent is not to divert him from his course but, on the contrary, to keep him on it. I have in mind questions or statements such as:

"You mentioned many children. What did you mean?"

"That feeling in your chest, can you describe it more fully?"

"It sounds as if you really hated it. Did you?"

"I wonder how you felt when she called you on the carpet."

"The way you talk about 'the old people up there' I get the idea that at times you count yourself in and at other times, out. Is that how it is — sometimes in and sometimes out?"

"I see you're seriously considering leaving home. Any ideas as to what you'll do then, assuming you don't get that job?"

Statements or questions like the above may fall into this category or into the one that follows. Sometimes we are the one who needs clarification, although we may impute this need to the interviewee. At other times both of us may require clarification. And in certain situations the truth of this may never be discerned.

Still another situation may arise, one in which we need further information — not to appease curiosity, but to understand more fully. We may feel that we need to hear more from the interviewee in order to remain within his frame of reference. The amount of questioning we engage in here will depend on our sensitivity to and our grasp of the situation. Unless we are very aware of what we are doing, our own needs may get in the way of the interviewee's. Much depends on how we word our inquiry and whether or not we interrupt his stream of talk, thought, or feeling. Knowing that I am not the most patient human being, I try to follow the rule of interjecting a question only if lack of comprehension of what has gone before would hamper my understanding what is to come.

"How long has your father been paralyzed?"

"I didn't quite understand what led you to change your job. Could you tell me a bit more about that?"

"I think I understand what your feelings were about Mary, but how does Phil come into it?"

"I wonder how you felt when Jim came home after the accident."

"Have you ever undergone surgery before?"

"Can I just stop you for a moment to ask whether you spoke with the principal?"

Finally, I may feel it necessary to ask something that may assist an interviewee who finds it hard to continue talking although he seems to have more to say. This can be tricky. The interviewee may simply be catching his verbal breath, and by questioning him, I may get him off the track. Undoubtedly risks are involved, but the right question at the right time may help the interviewee bridge an awkward gap or break a long and heavy silence.

"Is there anything else you'd like to discuss today?"

"I see you find it difficult to continue. Perhaps we could talk a bit more about your stay in the hospital. Would you like to do that?"

"I understand you went to the ball game but left in the middle. What happened?"

"Now that you have the results of those tests you took, I wonder whether they have affected your vocational plans."

"I don't know what to make of this silence, do you?"

"You said something about difficulties in the workshop when you came in. Are you interested in talking about that now?"

My battle with the question is over. I meant to dethrone it but not to drive it out of the palace. I intended to stimulate you to think about questions and their place in the helping interview. I feel very strongly on the issue and, I suppose, show it. Putting my ideas down on paper has been helpful to me. I hope it may prove helpful to you as well — whether you agree, disagree, or withhold judgment. If as a result of reading this chapter, you have become more aware of the questions you ask, communication has taken place.

CHAPTER SIX

Communication

In this chapter we shall discuss communication. In a sense we have been discussing it right along. Without communication there would be no interview. However, as we well know, there are interviews — even helping interviews — in which the communication is far from optimal. The interviewer's goal is to facilitate communication, but obstacles that impede, distort, or complicate it often arise. There are, obviously, various factors that can help or hinder communication. I have already stated some and hinted at others. In this chapter I shall include these factors within a framework that may render them more meaningful. Like much else in this book, such an approach is not original with me. However, I find it congenial, clear, and simple. It has worked better for me than any other framework I have tried; pragmatically speaking, I have found it to be true. This framework includes two basic concepts: defenses and values.

DEFENSES AND VALUES

The less defensive we as interviewers can become, the more we shall help our interviewees discard their defenses. Communication between us will improve as a consequence. The more we become aware of what our values are and the less we need to impose them on the interviewee, the more we shall help him become aware of his own values and retain, adapt, or reject them as he sees fit. Knowing my own values, I can state them. If I can accept them as a changing part of my changing self, I may be able to accept his as a changing part of his changing self. Some of these values of mine may remain constant for me, and some may for him; but I shall not be afraid to expose mine, nor shall I fear being exposed to his. He, in turn, may learn not to fear exposing his values or being exposed to mine because he will know that he is not being threatened. In such an atmosphere he may learn to describe his values without fear of being judged. He will not need to defend because he will not feel attacked. Perceiving no necessity to adjust to the interviewer's values, he may discover those he really believes in.

Some time ago I spoke with a young man who, looking back upon his school years, had this to say about one of his teachers:

"He was my teacher for three years in junior high school, and I gave him hell. I was a devil then and hated the guy. That's what I thought then, but it wasn't only hate. He didn't let me get away with a thing in class, and lots of times he'd keep me in after school to talk things over. He told me exactly how he felt, and I remember I told him lots of things. . . . I don't know why exactly . . . I think, because I trusted him. Now that I think of it, that teacher never told me he was right and I was wrong. He said there were things I was doing he couldn't allow, or something like that, and he told me why. I told him how I felt about the kids in the class and how boring school was. He listened to it. We never got to see eye to eye on lots of things, but we knew where we stood. I know now that I learned more from him in those talks than I did during four years in high school. I didn't know it then, but he taught me to think and to see what I was doing. After a while he had enough, I guess, and I don't blame him. He gave me up for lost, I suppose, and he'll never know how much he helped me. It took me years to find it out."

Whenever the interviewer says directly or indirectly to the interviewee, "You may not say this," he is using his value system to block communication. Whenever he states or implies, "I can't listen to this," he is telling the interviewee not to communicate, to be ashamed of himself, to keep silent. If the interviewer will not listen, who will? Whenever the interviewee says to himself, "I can't come out with this" or "He won't want to hear this," obstacles to good communication exist. They may be largely of his own making, but they may also reflect the interviewer's behavior. It is quite another matter if the interviewee can say to himself, "I know he won't like hearing this one bit, but I also know he can take it." We can never be certain, of course, just how the interviewee perceives us, whom he sees in us, or of whom he reminds him. The only choice open to us, it would seem, is to be as genuinely ourselves as possible and to behave as nondefensively as possible in the hope that eventually he will see us as we are.

Rogers (1961, Chapt. 17) has pointed out that our own need to evaluate, to confirm, or to deny constitutes a major obstacle to good communication. I am convinced that this is so. For example, if when the interviewee tells me that everyone at the meeting turned against him, I show interest in how he perceived the situation, I shall be opening the gates to communication. On the other hand, if I tell him that it surely wasn't so terrible, that he is exaggerating, or that he was probably at fault if people turned against him, I shall be closing those gates. In the former case my response will lead him to explore the situation as it appears to him. I may then be able to help him examine it further and clarify his role as well as his perceptions of others and theirs of him. In the latter case, my reply tells him in essence that he has misjudged the situation and that the fault may well have been his. He may consequently feel the necessity to defend himself against my judgment and thus fail to come to grips with the situation itself.

To take another example, if the interviewee tells me he liked a certain book and I tell him I did not, he will either refrain from examining just what he liked about the book or feel the need to defend his liking it. On the other hand, if I exhibit an interest in his view, he may feel encouraged to discuss the book and explore what he liked about it. Consequently, he may begin to learn something about himself, his likes and dislikes, his values. Having been respectfully listened to, he may wish to hear my views because he has become genuinely interested in my values — but as mine, not his. Our respective values may or may not be modified as a result, but at least we shall have learned how we both feel about the book.

Communication is not essentially better if I simply agree with the interviewee when he states that he likes a certain novel. We have really described nothing and learned nothing about each other's values. We do not know, in other words, what led each one to like the same book. One may have liked it because of the plot; the other because of the vivid characterization. Reasons for liking the same thing can be very diverse. Communicationwise, the fact of our mutual liking is far less significant than the fact that we have been enabled to express the reasons for it.

There exists a real possibility that as the result of such mutual describing, the perception of one or both partners will undergo change. For some people this offers a challenge; they regard it as a part of growing. For others it spells danger; for them change is threatening, and they cannot allow communication to be clear and direct. They will obstinately defend themselves against change. Their values will prove a reliable shield in warding off the threat.

Many interviewers who have learned not to fear revealing themselves have discovered that interviewees absorb this lesson from their examples. The interviewer can allow himself to describe how he perceives the interviewee's behavior without making the latter feel that he is being evaluated or categorized. The interviewer may say, for example: "I feel bored with that old story" or "The way you talk about it makes me feel that there is more to it than that" or "I feel slightly annoyed by those smiles; I wonder how you really and truly feel about me" or "I feel that you want me to tell you what is right for you, but I can't."

Authority as a Defense

At times the interviewer employs his authority as a defense, a barricade. "Teachers are never wrong," "The doctor knows best," and "Adults have more experience" are often convenient defenses. They won't solve the problem confronting the interviewee but serve to protect the interviewer from "attack" in the form of an honest search by the interviewee, a real coping with his situation. Confronted by a facade of superiority, the interviewee must defend himself as best he can. If he perceives it as the expression of the interviewer's values, he may either submit or emerge with a shield to defend his own values. Two formidable obstacles to communication will then prevail: the interviewer's use of authority and the interviewee's use of weapons to combat it.

I am not suggesting that our role — our function in society and in the life of the interviewee — has no relation to authority; it has. The issue is how we apply that authority in the helping interview and to what ends. While the interview is proceeding, are we indicating, implying, or stating: "This is not to be discussed," "That is a professional secret," "You'll just have to take my word for it," "I know best," "This is final; there is nothing to add"? When the interviewee is confronted with such attitudes, it is not surprising if he feels that he is being hemmed in and treated like an object. He may submit, learning thereby to depend on authority. He may rebel, resorting to a defense of his own. What will be absent is a free, open expression and exchange of ideas and feelings. Communication will have been obstructed.

The alternative is an atmosphere in which a sense of equality prevails — not equality of knowledge, experience, or professional skill, naturally, but equality of worth and dignity, with each human being fully respecting the other. Here no defensive shield is available to us, the interviewer; we are vulnerable. With nowhere to hide, we may come to light as a real person trying to help another real person. The interviewee will soon discover that we are neither all-powerful, all-wise, nor the embodiment of human virtue. The sooner he does, the better for him and our relationship. Seeing that we are not a closed book, he may permit himself to turn the pages of his own. He will find that the shields he brought with him as a result of habit and experience are not needed here. Since he will be confronting a true other, he will find that he can express his true self. For him, too, there will be no place to hide, but he will not be alone. Another will be there as he begins to cope with his own self.

Do we really possess the answers? Are we certain we are right? Are our conclusions necessarily correct just because they are ours? In an atmosphere in which equal meets equal our certainty may well have to give way to a mutual attitude of "Let's see" or "Let's try." This may be no more than provisional, but it will be understood by both, hence meaningful to both. Deprived of defensive shields, we have no alternative but to be flexible, to look at and respond to all aspects of a given situation. We may help the interviewee reach a decision. We may even be making it for him in a manner of speaking. But whatever we do, we shall be doing it with him, not to him. He will consider himself an equal, allowing himself to take from us what he chooses and to reject what is not for him.

Test Results as a Defense

Interviewers tend to use another defensive shield. Hiding behind diagnoses and test results, we lose sight of the person and in his stead see the category into which he has been placed. However, I think we are appreciating increasingly that diagnoses may err and that test results give only a part of the picture. Although more psychological and psychometric tests are available today than ever before, most are still in an experimental stage and can seldom if ever be relied on as conclusive. Even worse for us and our interviewees, equally qualified experts may arrive at different diagnoses, for test interpretations largely depend on the makeup of the psychologist interpreting them. This is a shaky shield indeed — which may explain why it is held on to with such tenacity at times. Whether we like it or not, the fact remains that even in medicine, which holds diagnosis nearly sacrosanct, specialists concurring in the diagnosis will frequently suggest opposite courses of treatment. In addition, medical opinion seems agreed today that unless the patient wishes to get well, little can be done for him. As in all effective helping relationships, the patient is at the center; we must reach him and reach out to him. Diagnoses and test results may keep the interviewee from himself. An honest, open, human confrontation will not.

Judging as a Defense

A final defense must be mentioned: judging the interviewee. It, too, constitutes an obstacle to open communication in that it encourages us to rationalize our behavior rather than come to grips with it. We judge the interviewee to be "uncooperative," "a troublemaker in the classroom," "aggressive," "submissive," "eccentric," etc. Consequently, we see him as such, and, more often than not, he will tend to see himself as such. But is this his real self, all of it or even a part? Or is this our perception of him, our perception at a given time and place and under given circumstances? Are we perhaps in error? Even if we are right, if we have "judged" him correctly, have we "judged" ourselves as well? May he not be acting this way because of us — because of his perception of us or his reaction to our perception of him?

Students who are attempting to listen to their taped interviews as nondefensively as possible often wonder whether they have judged the interviewee correctly or whether their judging was meaningful at all. Interviewees as well, hearing their own tapes, frequently begin to wonder if they have perceived the interviewer correctly and judged him fairly. It is amazing how much closer to each other the two partners in an interview can draw when they both lower their defensive armor. Then real coping occurs; and arguing, so frequently found in interviews, tends to disappear. By arguing I do not mean honest disagreement or an open clash of values. I mean misunderstandings, confusion, trying to get the upper hand, making a point regardless of whether it is being listened to, saying something for the record and not to the other.

I have found that the more obstacles to communication there are, the more arguing shows up. This should not surprise us, for arguing is bound to result from these obstacles. Each side holds on tightly to its own; it is give or take, not give and take. Gradually the interview comes to a halt. The session isn't really over, but it seems as if nothing more can be said or done. Interviewee and interviewer appear to be saying to each other: "This arguing isn't getting us anywhere so we may just as well stop. You can't listen to me, and I can't listen to you, so what's the use." It is useless, in fact. But even at this point if we can be honest enough to realize what has been going on and to express it, we may yet save the situation. "We've been kind of yelling at each other, and now it looks as if there is nothing more to say. I suppose we've gotten things off our chests, but I'm not sure whether we've gotten across to each other. Frankly, as the argument got hotter and hotter, I heard less and less of what you were saying; and I suppose it was the same with you. Why don't we just assume we've made a bad job of it and try again."

Dealing with Obstacles

There are ways — such as checking notes, listening to tapes, and discussing interviews with professional persons — whereby one can discover to what extent communication obstacles are present. These self-imposed tests and tasks, so to speak, are not foolproof. In any case, it is undoubtedly valid to say that communication obstacles exist to some degree in every interview. Our goal, as I perceive it, is not to eliminate them altogether, for our inability to achieve this might lead us to despair. It is, rather, to become aware of our behavior in interviews, to see where we may be creating obstacles, and to try to reduce these as much as possible, all the while recognizing that we remain humanly fallible. The five ways of reducing obstacles

I am about to discuss have helped me and a good many of my students.

Amount You Talk

If you tend to talk as much or even more than the interviewee, chances are that you are blocking communication from him to you. It is quite likely that you are acting as an authority, as the superior in the interview who must be respectfully listened to, and that the interviewee perceives you in this way. You may be lecturing the interviewee and not becoming sufficiently aware of his internal frame of reference while causing him to become too much aware of yours.

Should you find yourself talking very little — about 10 percent or less of the total talk — you may wish to look into this. Are there many pauses, awkward silences? Do you say so little because you are reluctant to get in the interviewee's way but find that in holding back you are getting in his way nonetheless? Do the two of you seem comfortable with the fact that you are talking so little, or does the atmosphere seem unnatural and tense to you both? If you find that the little you say enables the interviewee to release feelings and express ideas and at the same time enables you to go along with him, you may have achieved good rapport. The amount of talk is but one indication of what goes on in the interview and must be seen within the context of the entire process.

Interruptions

Do you tend to let the interviewee finish what he has to say, or do you often finish it for him and reply to that? Do you tend to interrupt him because you are quick to catch his intent and become impatient? Believing that you have heard many times in the past what he is now saying, do you become bored and cut him off? After your interruptions, what happens to the flow of the interview? An interruption creates a major communication obstacle. It cuts short communication that is actually taking place. Our motives may be the best: to show that we understand so well that we can finish the interviewee's sentence for him, to demonstrate our interest by interjecting

questions. Our motives notwithstanding, we are actually chok-
ing off what is coming our way, although we may sincerely
believe ourselves to be encouraging further flow.

At times interruptions lead to a form of duet; both partners
are talking at once — the one continuing with what he was
saying when interrupted and the other continuing to interrupt him. When we realize what is happening, we can probably do nothing better than stop and, if necessary, state
openly what has occurred. But this explanation should be very
brief lest it become, in turn, an interference. "Sorry, go ahead"
may suffice. At times the interviewee, well trained to look up
to "authority," may stop in his tracks as soon as we open our
mouth. Here we may have to say more: "Sorry I interrupted.
I was too quick on the trigger. Please go ahead; I'll have my
say when you're through."

We must become especially aware of interruptions by the
interviewee. These may well indicate that we have not understood him aright, that he has decided to add or amend, or that,
for one reason or another, he finds it difficult to continue
listening to us. Interviewer remarks such as "I'm talking
now so please listen" or "I've done you the courtesy of
listening to you so now please do me the courtesy of listening
to me" usually add insult to injury. The helping interview is
not an exercise in manners except insofar as we wish to use it
to teach manners. Whatever the case, if the interviewee inter-
rupts us and we wish to remove communication obstacles to
the greatest extent possible, sensitivity on our part to what is
going on may assist us to find the causes. If we really wish to
hear the interviewee, the best thing is to stop and listen. There
will always be time for us to have our say. Our need to talk,
unfortunately, is often greater than our ability to listen. This
is a very human failing, but since it creates obstacles to communication, it should be overcome.

Responses

Am I responding to what the interviewee has expressed or to
what, in my opinion, he should have expressed? In other words,
am I responding to his needs or to my own? Do my responses

enable him to express himself further? Are my responses clear? Am I getting across to him? Do my responses constitute additional obstacles to those he is already facing? In short, are my responses a help or a hindrance to the flow of his talk? We shall consider this aspect more fully in the next chapter.

Forces and Facets

Any topic discussed in an interview usually has several facets. Do I assist the interviewee to see, discuss, and cope with as many of these as possible? When a course of action is being considered, normally certain forces push the interviewee in one direction, and other forces pull him in another. This pushing and pulling may be going on at the same time. Am I helping the interviewee to explore all directions, or does my behavior impede his doing so? Do I place obstacles in the way of his exploring his own life space and perceptual field? We cannot always answer these difficult questions, but the posing of them itself may remove impediments to communication.

A Helpful Communication Test

In his well-known article "Dealing with Breakdowns in Communication — Interpersonal and Intergroup," written in 1951, Rogers (1961, Chapt. 17) referred to an interesting communication test which has since been frequently employed in human relations training and in various classroom situations. The test is challenging and difficult, but I have found that people value the learning experience involved and derive genuine satisfaction from it. Two or more persons are asked to discuss a topic on which they hold differing views. Each is allowed to say whatever he likes under one condition: before voicing his views, he must restate the ideas and feelings expressed by the person who spoke immediately preceding him and do so to that person's satisfaction. The assumption is that if I can tell you what you said and felt, then I heard and understood you. If I cannot, either I placed obstacles in the way or you did not make yourself sufficiently clear. Thus the test motivates the speaker to clarify his thinking and the listener to concentrate on what is being said rather than on the reply he will make.

The higher feelings rise in the discussion, obviously the harder it is to obey the rule. At times things reach such a point that a neutral is required. As each participant speaks, the neutral restates to that participant's satisfaction what he has said and felt before the next participant is allowed to speak. In the helping interview we may not always wish to restate the thoughts and feelings expressed by the interviewee, but if we are able to recapture his message to us in this manner, it will show that minimal communication obstacles are present. In other words, if I can provide an atmosphere in which you can release your feelings and ideas without interference from mine and if I can recognize these ideas and feelings as yours, showing you that I have heard, understood, and accepted them as yours, chances are that we are truly communicating and that obstacles are at a minimum. Furthermore, in such an atmosphere you will be receptive to the ideas and feelings I communicate to you. Thus the result will be a genuine interview.

WHEN INTERVIEWEE WON'T TALK

Interviewing does not consist of talk alone; there is nonverbal communication as well. However, if there is no talk at all, there may be no interview at all. "What shall I do if the interviewee won't talk or won't continue to talk?" one is often asked. I am certain that in most instances the interviewee will talk if really given the opportunity. I once met a young woman who wished to discuss her relationship with her husband. She insisted that he was the "silent type" and hardly ever spoke. We agreed that the three of us would meet. The husband talked — at least he attempted to — but each time he started, his wife would interrupt. Perceiving this, I could not help but smile. The young woman understood the smile and made a supreme effort to allow him to talk. When I last heard from her, she goodhumoredly volunteered the information that her husband was no longer the silent type and that she had learned a great deal about her own behavior.

It is not always as simple as this, I admit, but if the interviewee is interested in the interview, he will usually talk if we let him or encourage him a bit. On the other hand, he may not have wanted the interview and feels pushed into it by others, perhaps by ourselves. In that case it may be preferable for us to indicate that we understand and accept his reluctance, and then refrain from pushing him further. If and when he becomes ready, or "motivated," he will return and he will talk. Should he not return, it will not be because we consciously made the experience a threatening and unpleasant one. Not everyone wishes to be helped and not everyone can be helped in the helping interview. To have a sincere offer of help rejected is painful, but we must learn to accept this. We may even eventually learn to accept the fact that in situations in which we have "failed," another interviewer can succeed.

But what if the interviewee won't continue to talk? Here I am assuming that communication has taken place, that contact has been established. If the interviewee then stops, perhaps he has finished. Or maybe the interviewer has thrown obstacles into his path, the kind discussed above. Or perhaps the interviewee has come up against obstacles in himself that hinder him from going further. The response to the ensuing silence will depend upon the interviewer's perception of what is happening. I can only suggest possible ways to reopen communication.

"Is there anything else you wish to say?" (Interviewee shakes his head.) "All right, I'd just like to make one more comment. . . ."

"I see you find it difficult to continue. I wonder if your silence is connected with anything I've said."

"I don't quite know what to make of this silence. Perhaps there is something you find difficult to put into words."

"The last time we hit a silence like this, you said it was because of something I had done. How about this time?"

PREOCCUPATION WITH SELF

A basic factor in communication relates more to the interviewer's behavior than to the interviewee's. As the interview proceeds, you, the interviewer, may be asking yourself what to say or do next. This concern with your own role may so absorb your attention that you will not be genuinely listening to the interviewee. You will be preoccupied with that small voice inside that insists on knowing how to act next. This inner voice constitutes a clear obstacle to communication. It is not to be confused with the other inner voice that brings you closer to the world of the interviewee — that "third ear" with which you suddenly understand something haltingly expressed. The voice that insists on knowing what to do next is a block between you and your partner in the interview. It is concerned more with you than with him, more with the impression you will make on him than with the impressions he might make on you if you were listening and trying to understand with him.

Should you, then, not be concerned with what you are to do or say? Naturally you must be, but not consciously while the interviewee is expressing himself. When you really listen, almost inevitably a moment's silence will intervene between the interviewee's pausing and your carrying on. Whatever you say or do next will be unpremeditated. It may not be polished or carefully thought through, but it will be genuine. It will come forth spontaneously as the result of your having truly listened. At any rate, you will not have planned your action at the expense of having lost track of the interviewee. You will not sound like the "ideal" interviewer, but you may well sound like yourself. The ideal interviewer does not exist, but you do; and if the interviewee can sense the genuine, unplanned, spontaneous you, he will have an experience rare in our society. He might even dare to learn from this experience.

On the other hand, should the interviewee sense that we are occupied, not with what he is saying, but with our eventual response to it, this could be very harmful to the relationship between us. He might imbibe from this a lesson I doubt we wish him to learn: in the interview the important thing is not to be listened to but to be responded to. Were he to act on this conclusion, he would not listen to us either but instead would plan his responses. Perhaps this sounds absurd, but I have known it to happen.

When not stemming merely from lack of experience, this

preoccupation with self, I fear, has deep roots somewhere else. We are concerned with how we shall appear instead of being satisfied with what we are. We are concerned with demonstrating our role rather than revealing ourself; with being perceived as superior rather than behaving as an equal; with presenting a show of authority rather than letting our authority — if it exists at all — come through naturally in the ongoing exchange of ideas and feelings.

I reiterate my conviction that the interviewer's preoccupation with self at the expense of the interviewee creates a serious obstacle to communication. If we can accept ourselves as fallible, we shall err less. If we can learn to rely on our spontaneity, sensitivity, and basic common sense, we shall listen better and understand more. Our behavior influences that of the interviewee more than we know. Behaving openly ourselves, we shall encourage him to do likewise.

Providing Information Interviewee Needs

At this point I want to discuss an obstacle to communication that often is not perceived as such or is entirely overlooked. I am referring to certain aspects of the process involved in providing information to the interviewee.

First of all, however, let us note the following special circumstances. Sometimes when the interviewee asks the interviewer for information, the interviewer may not wish to furnish it because he thinks that the interviewee already possesses it or can easily obtain it by himself. For example:

Iee. Am I blushing?
Ier. Do you feel embarrassed?

Iee. Can you tell me whether this course is being offered next fall?
Ier. The new listings have just been published; you may wish to look them over.

In the first instance the interviewer may not have wished to reply either yes or no because he assumed that how the interviewee felt was more relevant than any information he could supply about the color of her cheeks. In the second example he may not have wanted to give a definite answer because he wished to encourage the interviewee to do for himself what he could easily do while gaining additional information in the process. However, the failure to provide certain types of information may create obstacles to communication.

In this major category of information that if provided may impel the interview forward and if withheld may block smooth progress, first I shall discuss information requested by the interviewee. This is knowledge that the interviewer possesses and the interviewee does not have but feels he needs and cannot obtain by his own resources. In such situations a straightforward reply is helpful. In the following examples the mere reflection of feeling or the verbalized recognition of the fact that the interviewee is seeking information would not have sufficed:

Iee. Did you speak to Mr. Adams the way we agreed?
Ier. Yes, I did. He and I had quite a talk. There are some things on which you see eye to eye, but there are others that make it hard to believe both of you are speaking of the same incidents.

Iee. Do you know whether I got the scholarship?
Ier. No, not yet; but as soon as I know, I'll tell you.

Iee. Will I feel the operation?
Ier. You shouldn't feel anything during the operation, but there will be some pain afterwards for a few days. We'll try to make you as comfortable as possible, but you won't feel very comfortable at first.

Iee. Do they know at the factory that I was at X hospital?
Ier. To the best of my knowledge they don't. I wonder how you feel about that.

Iee. If I should need you while you're on vacation, will I be able to get in touch with you?
Ier. No, you won't, but Miss C. will be available during my absence. I see you have mixed feelings about my going on vacation. You want me to go away and rest, but you want me nearby as well.

In some of the above examples the interviewer goes beyond providing the requested information. He relates it to the interviewee's internal frame of reference and thereby shows his interest in what the information may mean to the interviewee or how it may affect him. When appropriate, this seems to me as helpful a response as can be made.

The interviewer may also profitably provide information that the interviewee has not requested. He may do this to reduce tension. On occasion the interviewee may wish to ask but may neither dare to nor know how to go about it. Perhaps the interviewee may not even be cognizant of the fact that if he were provided with some necessary information, he would feel more relaxed. All the following interviewer statements exemplify this approach:

"The money hasn't come through yet; I know you must be anxious."

"I'm the person who meets with the parents of the children staying with us. You can reach me here by phone, and we can make an appointment whenever you feel you wish to discuss matters relating to Peggy's stay. Once a month there is a meeting of all the parents at which. . . ."

"Mr. S. is sick today. I'm pinch-hitting for him. I'll be happy to talk with you unless you prefer waiting for his return."

"I saw you copying from Joe, and your two tests are practically identical. I just wanted you to know that I know before we go any further."

"I have the impression you are wondering whether I know more about you than you have told me. As a matter of fact, I do. Mr. D. told me of your illness, and he wanted me to inform you that he had done so. I'm glad I know because this enables me to understand the situation better. I wonder how you feel about it . . . my knowing, I mean."

"I am free till noon so we have plenty of time, and you can tell me everything you wish without hurrying."

One last point. I, the interviewer, may remove a communication obstacle by telling the interviewee frankly what I am doing or propose to do and for what reasons. This will eliminate any aura of mystery surrounding my status and indicate that here in the helping interview he can be equally frank. Some examples:

> "I should like to write and ask them about your records; then we'll be able to compare. O.K.?"

> "I won't be in next Tuesday because I have an earlier commitment. How about Thursday instead?"

> "I'll give you the injection now. It will hurt very little. Then you'll have to lie down for ten minutes or so till we can go on with the examination. No cards up my sleeve, so you can relax now."

Occasionally I may be unable to furnish certain information because I do not have it and may wish to inform the interviewee of this fact. For example: "I can't tell you about summer camp for Janet yet because the committee hasn't reached its decision. We'll just have to wait."

CHAPTER SEVEN

Responses and Leads

In this final chapter the focus is on responses and leads. I shall deal with those already mentioned but not placed into the present context, as well as with others not yet touched upon. Inasmuch as the number of possible responses and leads is all but limitless, I shall not even attempt to be comprehensive but shall merely consider those most frequently used. Although I shall not pretend to be impartial, I shall try to be fair.

The difference between response and lead cannot be unmistakably defined, for a response may change into a lead, and a lead may be meant as a response and interpreted as such. However, there is a basic difference in the way individual interviewers lead and respond, and this will become evident when one examines the particular style each interviewer develops and finds most congenial. Extracts from random interviews may present an erroneous picture. The extracts I shall cite, therefore, are for the purpose of identifying and analyzing the particular response or lead and will not deal with interviewer style. Developing a style is a task each interviewer, if interested, must undertake for himself in a manner least threatening and most helpful to him.

The essential difference between response and lead is denoted in the definitions of the two words themselves. When I respond, I speak in terms of what the interviewee has expressed. I react to the ideas and feelings he has communicated to me with something of my own. When I lead, I take over. I express ideas and feelings to which I expect the interviewee to react. Leading, of course, may also be in response to what has already occurred in the interview or to the last statement made by the interviewee; however, it generally involves a quite different attitude. When leading, I make use of my own life space; when responding, I tend more to utilize the life space of the interviewee. Interviewer responses keep the interviewee at the center of things; leads make the interviewer central. Philosophically speaking, those interviewers who usually employ more responses than leads seem to believe that the interviewee has it within himself to find the way. Those who tend to lead seem to act on the conviction that the interviewee needs the way pointed out to him. It is evident that much blurring and overlapping exist here. The interviewer's intentions are important, but the way the interviewee perceives them is decisive. For each interviewer there is the forest and there are the trees. The forest is his overall style; the trees, his leads and responses. In this chapter we shall examine only the trees in the hope that this may help us eventually to look at the forest more closely and see it more clearly.

Some years ago Robinson (1950) presented a gradated list of responses and leads ranging from what he termed most nondirective to most directive, i.e., from those most centered in the interviewee's internal frame of reference to those least centered in it. I shall base my model on his approach while keeping clear of the nondirective-directive controversy (Rogers, 1942), which, I submit, belongs to the past. (For elaboration on this point see Rogers, 1961; Bugental, 1965; Beck [ed.], 1966.) We realize today that a very directive lead may be helpful in a situation in which neither recognition nor reflection of feeling is helpful, and we know the reverse is true as well. In addition, enough research evidence is available (Fiedler, 1950, 1951) to show that it is the interviewer as a human being whom the interviewee perceives above and beyond any theory of interviewing the interviewer advocates or any leads and responses he employs.

One additional point must be stressed. I am convinced that it is a mistake to assume that the interviewer who talks little and uses more responses than leads is passive or that one who talks much and leads often is active. Listening with understanding is not, as I see it, in the least passive. Familiarizing oneself with the interviewee's life space is activity indeed. An interviewer who talks and leads extensively may not be active in this sense at all. What makes the difference is the interviewer's degree of involvement with the interviewee — with his thoughts and feelings, his hopes and fears, his perceptions of the world. Thus the interviewer can be very actively involved and say almost nothing or he can be passive though speaking and leading most of the time. The question remains, With whom is the interviewer most involved? To repeat, the interviewer who is involved largely with himself is active or passive in a way clearly unlike that of the interviewer who is involved primarily with the interviewee.

Blurs, overlappings, and ambiguities notwithstanding, responses and leads will be described in a certain order. Not from "good" to "bad" or from "right" to "wrong" but not haphazardly or nonevaluatively either. I do find that the more we tend to use the responses and leads listed last in this chapter, the less we are truly taking into account the interviewee and his world. The more we employ the responses and leads listed at the beginning, the less likely we are to impose ourselves and our world on him. This is not a clear-cut issue. It may not even be a matter of consistency. However, all of us follow a distinct trend that is expressed in our style whether we are aware of it or not. It is our way of being human. There are many such ways, and I have not concealed the one I feel to be most helpful.

INTERVIEWEE-CENTERED RESPONSES AND LEADS
Silence

I have discussed silence previously in another context. It is listed here first because it can be a response, although this fact is frequently overlooked. The response is nonverbal, of course, but can express a great deal. A gesture on the interviewer's part may communicate: "Yes, I'm with you, go on" or "I'm waiting, sensing that you have not finished" or "You've said that before; I'm beginning to get bored." Our gestures mean much; so do our glances and the way we move about in our chair. Just as words have meaning, silence has meaning. Through it both partners in the interview may be drawing closer, sharing something; or silence may show them just how wide the gulf between them really is. Silence may point up misunderstanding. It may be neutral or very empathic. It may be the result of confusion. It can say, "We have really finished but haven't yet admitted it." As a deliberate response, silence implies that the interviewer has decided to say nothing, regarding this as the most helpful thing he can offer at this point. He decides not to interfere verbally, but he is there in the interview, and his presence is felt by the interviewee. It is as if the interviewer were saying: "You know I am listening. The best way in which I can be of help right now, I believe, is to keep quiet. I am not afraid of the silence because I feel that this is what you want." Often his gestures will communicate this to the interviewee quite clearly.

Unless the interviewer is very sure of his ground, he should avoid extensive silences; a minute of meaningful silence is quite lengthy. If it is true, as the proverb would have it, that words are silver but silence is gold, then we ought to value silence as a response more than we do. Perhaps we can become more aware of our own feelings about silences in the interview and determine how we use them. As an intentional response prop-

erly utilized, silence can be an important facet of the experience the interviewee takes away with him, saying to himself,
"Here I was really listened to."

"*Mm-hm*"

This is a verbal response. Though not a word, it is clearly an
uttered sound. It is generally considered to indicate permissive-
ness on the part of the interviewer, expressing, "Go on, I'm
with you; I'm listening and following you." However, its
usage is not quite so restricted. By an "mm-hm" the interviewer may instead indicate approval of what the interviewee
is saying or of how he is going about handling his situation. It
may tell the interviewee that the interviewer likes what he is
doing and, therefore, encourage him to continue in that direction. "Mm-hm" may also at times suggest criticism, as though
to say: "So that's how you feel!" or "So that's what you're
thinking!" In other situations it may imply suspended judgment, as if the interviewer were saying, "Well, let's see what
you are going to add; I want to wait a bit."

The possibilities are manifold. "C'est le ton qui fait la
musique." This is true for all responses and leads including
"mm-hm." We may wish to become aware of how we use
"mm-hm," that is, if we use it, and study how the interviewee
interprets it. In the following excerpts it has various meanings:

IEE. I don't know what would be best for me; I keep going back
    and forth and don't seem to be able to make up my own mind.
IER. Mm-hm.

IEE. I don't like the way this agency functions. You people promise
    a lot, but it's just words with nothing behind them.
IER. Mm-hm.

IEE. If my mother would only stop picking on me everything
    would be all right. She doesn't pick on my brother, just on me.
IER. Mm-hm.

In the first instance the interviewer meant to be permissive,
to let the interviewee explore her own indecisiveness. In the
second, he felt disapproving of the criticism expressed. In the

last, he wished to wait and see what would develop. Now let's look at the following examples. When the interviewer examined her feelings, she concluded that in the first instance she felt approving and in the second, disapproving. How the interviewees perceived her is not clear.

IEE. Last month I followed your suggestion, and it worked. I managed much better with the budget, and there was less drinking.
IER. Mm-hm.

IEE. I've tried the hearing aid — I really have — but I can't get used to it. So I brought it back; let someone else have it.
IER. Mm-hm.

Other responses might have been used, but this is begging the question — other responses can always be employed. The "mm-hm" seems noncommittal on the interviewer's part but does not necessarily imply that he refuses to commit himself. That may come later. Meanwhile, he wishes to let the interviewee know by uttering this sound that he is prepared to listen further. Although apparently a nonjudgmental sound, "mm-hm" has many nuances, which the interviewer may be aware of and which his partner will perceive correctly or incorrectly. It may be hard to believe that a litle "mm-hm" is open to such a wide range of meaning and interpretation; but a careful perusal of interviews will show, I believe, that this is the case.

Restatement

Now, at last, the interviewer speaks. He uses actual words, but they are those of the interviewee. Restatement can be accomplished in various ways, but the rationale is the same: to serve as an echo, to let the interviewee hear what he has said on the assumption that this may help him, encourage him to go on speaking, examining, looking deeper. When the interviewer utilizes restatement, his own perceptual field either does not enter the picture at all or enters it to a very small extent. Restatement communicates to the interviewee: "I am listening to you very carefully, so carefully, in fact, that I can restate what you have said. I am doing so now because it may

help you to hear yourself through me. I am restating what you have said so that you may absorb it and consider its impact, if any, on you. For the time being, I am keeping myself out of it."
   Restatement can be effected in four basic ways:

1. Restating exactly what has been said without even changing the pronoun the interviewee has used.

IEE. I felt cold and deserted.
IER. I felt cold and deserted.

2. Restating exactly, changing only the pronoun.

IEE. I felt cold and deserted.
IER. You felt cold and deserted.

I find the latter form more helpful than the first. The exact repetition, pronoun and all, seems to me artificial and affected. If the interviewer is to keep himself out of it to that extent, the use of a tape recorder would be preferable, in my opinion.

3. Restating part of what has been said, the part the interviewer feels to be most significant and worth having the interviewee hear again:

IEE. So Joe and Mike and Chick ganged up on me, and before I knew what was going on, they knocked me down and ran.
IER. They ganged up on you, knocked you down, and ran.

4. Restating in summary fashion what the interviewee has said. This is a selective process. As he selects, the interviewer does use his own perceptual field, of course. However, he keeps himself emotionally and intellectually uninvolved and simply summarizes what he has heard. At times this results in his stressing one aspect of what the interviewee has just stated more than another and thereby goes beyond pattern three above and also, technically, beyond restating. We have come a long way from the tape recorder now. Contrast the following two examples:

IEE. I just couldn't tell him because we were never alone — the guys may have known what was up or . . . I don't know. All I know is that whenever I tried to tell him, there were people around;

and I just couldn't tell him then . . . what with all of these people. . . .

IER. You couldn't get him alone long enough to tell him.

IEE. When I got home that night . . . it was just awful. . . . At first I saw things blurred. Then things began to dance before my eyes, and then I could just feel that I was seeing less and less. I closed my eyes and reopened them. It was as if a gray curtain had descended all over the world; the world I knew collapsed that night.

IER. A curtain descended on the world you had known, and it collapsed all about you. You had gone blind.

It is possible, of course, to employ restatement in other ways — sarcasm or disbelief, for example.

IEE. I didn't do it.

IER. You didn't do it!

However, at present I shall deal, not with this interviewer-centered type of response, but with one in which the interviewee is kept central.

Clarification

Clarification is commonly understood to mean the interviewer's clarification for the interviewee of what the latter has said or tried to say. There is another side to the coin, but let us look first at this one, which has two possible designs:

1. The interviewer remains very close to what his partner has expressed but simplifies it to make it clearer. It is then, of course, up to the interviewee to decide whether this response has been helpful, whether it really clarified what he had in mind. For example:

IEE. The only thing that's clear to me is that I'm all mixed up. I want to try, but I can't. I want to be strong, but I'm acting weak. I want to make up my own mind, but I'm letting everybody sway me in every direction. It's one big mess. . . .

IER. You see quite clearly that you are mixed up and not doing what you wish to be doing.

2. The interviewer in his own words tries to clarify for the interviewee what the latter has had difficulty in expressing clearly. The interviewer submits a tentative synthesis of the interviewee's verbalized ideas and feelings for his approval, amendment, or rejection. It is as though the interviewer were translating the interviewee's words into a language more familiar to them both.

IEE. I'm not sure whether it was really nice that he came. It was friendly and kind and generous on his part, but I don't deserve it if he did it for me — and if he didn't do it for me, I'm still glad he came because really I don't deserve it. But that's how he is, and I couldn't get anything out of him. I couldn't even tell him how I feel. I got all confused. . . .

IER. You couldn't express to him how undeserving of his attention you feel.

IEE. It's easy to get used to being crippled, but you never get used to it. It's not clear, I know, but I can't make it any clearer. Do you get what I mean?

IER. I understood you to say that it is possible to manage as a crippled person, but it never quite feels the way it used to feel before. . . .

IEE. That's right. You can manage alright; that's simple enough. It's the other thing you never get used to — remembering and comparing and. . . .

The other side of the coin of clarification concerns the need of the interviewer to have things clarified for him. This aspect of clarification as a response is often overlooked entirely or else glossed over. Hence it needs pointing up. The interviewer cannot be expected to understand everything. He is humanly fallible, and it will help the interviewee to know that the interviewer realizes and accepts this. Such an attitude will facilitate communication.

IEE. He just threw me for a loop when. . . .

IER. I'm sorry — my English is still not very good — what did you say he threw?

The interviewee explains, and the interview continues. In this case the question was a genuine search for clarification, not mere flippancy, and rapport was thereby improved. Here are some more examples:

Iee. . . . and she said she meant it, but it didn't sound too kosher to me.

Ier. I thought that "kosher" refers to dietary laws. What did you mean by using it the way you just did?

Iee. You'd go crazy, too, if you lived in a house like mine. You couldn't stand it either. You wouldn't think any more of it than I do.

Ier. (*in a light, almost jesting manner*) You are imputing to me all sorts of thoughts and feelings about your home. Honestly, I don't know what it is like. I think I know how *you* feel about it, but perhaps you could describe it a little so that I can try to understand what upsets you so about goings-on there.

Reflection

This is a very difficult response to achieve. To reflect the feelings and attitudes of the interviewee demands deeply empathic listening and understanding. To serve as a mirror in which the interviewee can see his feelings and attitudes reflected requires a facility in recognizing and verbalizing those feelings and attitudes. When restating, the interviewer tells the interviewee what he has said. When reflecting, he verbalizes what the interviewee feels. Reflection should not be confused with interpretation, which will be discussed shortly. Reflection consists of bringing to the surface and expressing in words those feelings and attitudes that lie behind the interviewee's words. The interviewer echoes feelings not expressed as such by the interviewee but clearly sensed by the interviewer from what the other has said. The interviewer perceives these feelings and verbalizes them. Functioning like a mirror or an echo, the interviewer adds nothing of his own except — and this is all-important — his sensitivity and empathic interest, which enable him to put into words what the interviewee has meant affectively but stated intellectually or descriptively. In a manner of speaking, the interviewer acts like a very attentive hostess who senses, understands, and expresses the wishes of her guest when he hesitates to state them openly because he does not know whether this would be appropriate to the situation.

When reflecting, the interviewer neither guesses nor assumes. He voices what is there behind the word content and brings it to the fore as the emotional content, which has been present all the time but unexpressed by the interviewee. This in itself is hard to accomplish. The possibility of the following complication as well should be recognized: The reflection presented may be distorted and consequently rejected by the interviewee. In this case it was not reflection but another response, probably interpretation. However, even true reflection may be rejected by the interviewee when he perceives it as threatening. Therefore, it is not always easy to be certain that your response was indeed reflection. Consideration of the interview as a whole will usually help you ascertain this. I shall hazard this general rule: True reflection will be accepted by the interviewee because it simply consists of putting into words the feeling tone of what he just said. Or, to put it another way, what the interviewee verbally expressed was accompanied by an affective message that the interviewer received and then translated into words, thus in a way completing the interviewee's communication. The following examples will illustrate:

IEE. I was fired yesterday . . . general layoff . . . after all those years at the plant . . . No idea what to do next.

IER. After many years of steady employment you are jobless now, and you feel totally bewildered.

IEE. I just can't take it any longer and must do something.

IER. You're completely fed up and feel you've got to find a way out.

IEE. It's so hard knowing she's in the hospital and that there's nothing, absolutely nothing, I can do.

IER. You feel anxious and entirely helpless right now.

IEE. You're listening to me alright, but that doesn't do me any good.

IER. You feel that I'm paying attention to what you're saying but that this doesn't get you any closer to solving your problems.

IEE. If it had been my sister who had done that, my mother wouldn't have said a thing. It's never been any different.

IER. You feel your mother has always discriminated against you, and you resent it.

Iᴇᴇ. Well, I don't know . . . treated us differently. . . . I suppose you're right. I must have felt the discrimination right along; but when you said it, my first impulse was to come to Mother's defense.

Here the interviewee at first found it hard to accept the feeling tone of her own words. In the following excerpt the interviewee rejected the affective content of his words:

Iᴇᴇ. You have the right to do what you like. I don't care. Just don't give me all that bull about wanting to help. You don't have to . . . but you don't want to, and that's different.

Iᴇʀ. You feel quite angry with me right now.

Iᴇᴇ. No, I don't. You have every right. . . .

When the interviewer uses reflection, he responds not to his own inner frame of reference but solely to the feeling tone of the interviewee. Thus in the last example the interviewer reflected the interviewee's anger instead of reacting to his assertion that he, the interviewer, did not want to help. Nor, of course, did the interviewer dispute the assertion. He believed that sufficient evidence to the contrary existed but that to bring it out would be harmful at this point because the interviewee's deep anger, not cold facts, was at issue. This fact the interviewer was prepared to face, though his partner was not as yet. Later on when the interviewee could accept and explore his anger, he himself recalled the instances of help and began to understand what his anger had really been about.

Interpretation

Now, at long last for those who have missed it, the interviewer's frame of reference comes into focus. In all the responses so far, he has not expressed himself. If he has spoken at all, he has restricted himself to verbalizing what the interviewee has said or felt. This limitation of self is constricting for many interviewers. They wish to get across to the interviewee on their own terms, in their own personal way. To keep silent, say "mm-hm," restate what has been said, or reflect the feeling tone of the interviewee is not enough for them; and to some it is downright uncongenial. Personally I like these classical, nondirective responses and am convinced that interviewees find them helpful when the interviewer feels at ease with them and does not merely employ them as a technique. To my mind, the greatest merit of these responses is that they are, they are bound to be, interviewee-centered. Using them, we respond to him. It is his internal frame of reference that is all-important.

At this point in our discussion the emphasis shifts. The interviewer's frame of reference makes its appearance and, as the discussion proceeds, gradually takes over. We move slowly but surely from responses to leads. We are bringing ourselves onstage. The danger is obvious — that we take over at the expense of the interviewee; that we perform instead of him. We may end up enjoying this role so much we do not realize that we have turned him off; that we have put him into the audience, so to speak; that we have made of the interviewee-subject a spectator-object.

Interpretation is of two kinds. The first is based on the internal frame of reference of the interviewee; the second, on the internal frame of reference of the interviewer. When I interpret what I have understood from the interviewee's communication to me in terms of his life space, I am responding to him. On the other hand, when I interpret it in terms of my own life space, I have crossed the Rubicon and am expecting to have him respond to me. I am beginning to lead. This distinction is often overlooked but ought not to be. It makes quite a difference whether I translate in terms of how things seem to him or how they seem to me. The Rubicon is a narrow river, but for Caesar it was immense. In the examples of interpretation that follow, interviewer responses gradually move in the direction of leads; the frame of reference shifts from interviewee to interviewer.

IEE. It doesn't matter too much either way. I can get a babysitter for Tuesday if that's more convenient.

IER. I hear you saying that you can come on either day but that Tuesday involves getting a sitter. Thursday is quite convenient for me, so let's make it Thursday. Is that alright?

Iee. I haven't had to look for a job in such a long time that I'm sort of overwhelmed by the prospect. I can't quite see myself looking for employment.

Ier. I understand you to say that, being used to steady employment right along, you find it difficult to shift over, to see yourself as unemployed and having to act accordingly. It is hard to shift roles in this way and to realize that it is *you* all the while.

Iee. . . . I can't cut down on sports. . . . Everyone's been piling on the homework lately, and it's just too much.

Ier. You seem to be saying that the teachers are to blame when you don't do all your homework because they give too much and you cannot be flexible about your sports activities.

Iee. The truck's been coming late every week this past month, and they haven't been giving me as much work as they used to. I've got the same expenses, though, and you people ought to make good the difference. After all, it's your trucks and all that. . . .

Ier. No one else has complained. I'll look into the truck service and the work deliveries, but I'm wondering whether the work satisfies you the way I thought it did.

Iee. My older brothers are all working, and my big sister is married and out of the house. So Mother and Dad pick on me because there's no one else around to pick on. I bet they didn't treat the others that way when they were my age. It's not right.

Ier. You find it hard to be the baby of the family.

Iee. You never know exactly what people are telling you when you can't hear well. When you've got your back turned, well . . . then you don't know at all, and they're bound to be talking about you because they know you can't make it out. That's why I don't want the hearing aid. It would only make things worse. Then they wouldn't just guess, they would know, and I'd be sunk. Everyone would take advantage. . . .

Ier. You're quite suspicious of people, I notice. I wonder whether you realize that you may be causing the very results you fear. Your behavior would antagonize me, too, if I didn't know better.

Explanation

An explanation is a descriptive statement. It may include evaluative overtones — whether intended as such or not — which may be sensed by the interviewee. The interviewer may utilize explanation as a lead — in structuring the interview, for example — or as a response to interviewee statements and questions. As it is descriptive in character, explanation should be neutral in tone. It says that this is how things are. It implies that we must accept the way things are and behave accordingly. It tends to be impersonal, logical, matter-of-fact.

Not all interviewers employ explanation to the same degree. Some hesitate to use it until the interviewee is ready to assimilate it, when it is often superfluous. Other interviewers feel that neutral explanation can help the interviewee approach reality or remain within its bounds. Having provided an explanation, some make it a practice to ascertain whether what they have explained has been understood in the way they intended; others take this for granted. Explanation in the interview may be divided into four categories: orientation to situation, behavior, causes, and interviewer's position.

Orientation to Situation

IER. Whatever goes on in this room stays right here, as far as I'm concerned. Here you can feel free to say whatever you like in any way you want to say it. I'll try to help you understand and decide in which direction you want to go.

IER. We have two programs at our rehabilitation center. One is for those who sleep in; the other, for those who prefer to go home every afternoon. The first program is longer because we have more time available. The other is less intensive but enables the person to be with his family in the evenings. . . .

IER. I'm not the principal. I'm the school counselor, but Mr. G. asked me to meet with you. Requests like yours are turned over to me as I have more time at my disposal than the principal. I hope you won't mind discussing it with me. I shall, of course, pass on any decision we reach to Mr. G.

IER. I'm afraid I haven't made myself very clear. The doctor will see you but only after we have the results of these tests. He is busy, but he is not indifferent. He couldn't even begin to help you without knowing what the tests indicate. As soon as we have the results, I shall arrange an appointment for you.

IER. I suppose that's true. In class I do lose my temper at times. We have forty students, so there you are one out of forty. But now I have time just for you, and I don't think I'll lose my temper. I really want to find out what happened at home last night — not because I'm nosy, but because I'd like to help if I can. I understand it all started when. . . .

Explanation of Behavior

IER. Why don't you call me Fred, and I'll call you John. I like first names much better, and I do have trouble remembering family names.

IER. I want to hear what you have to say about it, but the fact is that Miss J. asked me to see you because she feels that your behavior in class disrupts her lessons. She says you either interrupt whoever is speaking or talk to one of your neighbors. She says you just can't keep still.

IER. I'm going to take a blood sample now so that we can test to what extent you are anemic. It won't hurt me a bit and you very little, and it'll help us both to know what we're doing.

IER. You're behaving in here just like that, too. You punch holes into my arguments but won't reveal your own. I don't share your husband's anger, but I'm beginning to see how he must feel.

IER. Your behavior does seem childish — wanting to be taken care of, finding it hard to stand on your own two feet; finding it easier to play than to work. There's more to it than that, of course, but that's the picture I get. I'm not saying whether it's good or bad but only describing how it strikes me.

IER. I don't know if my explanation is the correct one, but you did say that your father's behavior had changed lately, that he didn't spend as much time at home as he used to, and that your mother said there was another woman to whom he'd become attached. This is obviously hard for you to accept, but it may just possibly be true.

Explanation of Causes

IEE. I'm usually quite punctual, but now that you've pointed it out, I see I have been coming late to almost every one of our meetings. I don't get it. Do you?

IER. When punctual people come late time after time, the explanation may be that they are not too anxious to come. They may want to and yet not want to. The wanting to and not wanting to may conflict inside, resulting in latecoming. There may be another explanation, but what do you think of this one as relating to you?

IEE. . . . I want you to tell me why I'm afraid of you.

IER. Well, you've indicated several times that I remind you of your mother, and, as I recall it, you were afraid of her at times.

IEE. It's because I'm blind that people treat me like that — feeling sorry for me and keeping their distance. That's what the travel instructor said they did, and you can't deny it.

IER. No, I can't deny that being blind is tough on you, but I do feel that the cause of your trouble is not so much your blindness as how you relate to it: how you think and feel about being blind. This is the real cause, as I see it.

IEE. O.K., I'll say it: you hate me because of my black skin — because I'm colored and you're white.

IER. To the very best of my knowledge about myself, this is not true. I do dislike you at times but for an entirely different reason: because I feel you aren't treating me as an equal. You act superior and defiant and hostile. You keep well hidden what's underneath that, but when it does come through, I like it fine. So, you see, I reject your explanation. I see it as a defense. You need to be hostile to me because you must assume that I am hostile to you. As for me. . . .

Explanation of Interviewer's Position

IER. I'd like you to know what my stand is because it will probably influence the board. It is that we should take your son back but on a trial basis only. I'm still not sure that this is the best place for him. I know, however, that it will be hard to find something better and so think we should all give him and ourselves another chance — but a limited one, in order to be fair to all concerned.

Iee. . . . but why won't you talk to Miss M. about it? You're the school counselor, and she sent me to see you. So why won't you go talk to her?

Ier. My position is really very simple. If and when Miss M. wants to discuss the matter with me, I shall be ready to do so. I feel that after all that has happened, it would be better for you to talk with her. After that, the three of us can talk things over, should both of you wish that. You and I have met several times so that I could try to help you clarify things for yourself. I think we've done that. I know my position irritates you, and I'm very sorry for that; but honestly I can't act otherwise.

Iee. I can't understand how you people can allow a man like Mr. T. to work around here. He's rude and coarse and should be receiving help himself instead of trying to give it to others.

Ier. It's the policy of our agency — and I endorse it fully — that anyone who comes to us has the right to like or dislike whomever he comes in contact with. On the other hand, such likes and dislikes cannot be discussed with other workers of the agency as this might lower morale and lead to shopping around by clients. So I'll have to ask you to stop discussing Mr. T. and pass on to something we can fruitfully talk about.

You may wish to determine whether all the above excerpts are as descriptive in character and as neutral in tone as they might be.

INTERVIEWER-CENTERED LEADS AND RESPONSES

Encouragement

I suppose that pretty much everything we do in the helping interview we do to encourage the interviewee in one way or another. Our attitude, our approach, our responses — all are meant to support and strengthen him in his efforts to change in a direction meaningful and worth while for him. We wish to assist him in coming closer to reality and to his own self in order that he may explore his present situation and determine his future goals. Our slightest "mm-hm" is meant to spur him on. It tells him: "That's it. Go on. You're on your way. I'm with you. I care." Our mere desire to be of help is meant to support. The way we perform our job is meant to stimulate and strengthen determination. This manner of encouraging is an integral part of our philosophy. Like empathy it is not stated in words; but if it is present in us, the interviewee will sense it. If it is not, our saying that it is will not make it so nor deceive him into believing that it is.

Now, however, we shall discuss encouragement of a different sort — a type of lead (at times it is a response) in which encouragement is verbally and openly expressed. What encourages another person? We do not really know. Is he encouraged when we tell him that others suffer more than he does and that they somehow learn to make the best of things? Is he encouraged when we say that time is a great healer and that in a short while the world will seem a more cheerful place to him? Is he encouraged when we aver that we shall support him just as long as he feels he needs us — the implication being that he can lean on us because we are strong and he is weak? Whether or not he is fundamentally encouraged and strengthened, we do not know.

These questions I believe to be of basic importance. Every interviewer finds operational answers to them. My stand, I trust, is made clear in the chapter on philosophy. It necessarily colors my approach throughout this book, particularly regarding the leads to be discussed (we shall be concerned mostly with leads from now on). These leads are in general usage because the assumption is that they are helpful. Undoubtedly they sometimes are. Nevertheless, I have strong reservations about them simply because they tend to push and pressure the interviewee from the outside, from the frame of reference of someone else — a someone who is looked upon and sees himself as superior, as an authority figure. These leads may be internalized by the interviewee and thus serve to strengthen him; on the other hand, they may not. He may pay lip service to our various attempts to help, feeling cornered by them instead of strengthened or really helped, and wishing nothing more than to escape the situation as unscathed as possible. In the last resort, I suppose, the effect of leads on the interviewee depends on the person he is, the person he perceives us to be, and the person he feels we believe he can become.

In leading we must make sure that we are aware we are doing so and that we know whom we are leading and to what end. We must be prepared to retreat once we realize that we have not been helpful. Most important, we must lead in such a way, if we must lead at all, that the interviewee can release himself from our grasp, if he so chooses, without feeling he has hurt or offended us. We must keep in mind that in leading: we encourage the other to be led; we tell him he cannot get there on his own, not yet anyway; we foster dependency, at least for the time being; we assume the responsibility, for the moment at any rate. All this has a cumulative effect. Therefore, if we must lead, we ought to take the consequences of our actions into account. The caveat stated, I can proceed.

Assurance-Reassurance

We use assurance or reassurance as a lead to tell the interviewee in words that we believe in his capability to act and overcome obstacles, to face up to his situation successfully. In effect, we are also showing him that we can see farther ahead than he, that he can safely place his trust in us, that it is up to him to act but that he requires a little pat on the back from us to help him on his way. Thus we indicate that he needs an external influence to keep him going or get him started and that this we shall provide. The following examples range from mild to heavy reassurance, openly expressed:

IEE. I can't face him.

To this different interviewers may reply:

IER. You haven't tried; it may not be as bad as you think.
IER. I'm not so sure you can't; I rather suspect you can.
IER. Can't you? That's one man's opinion; this man thinks otherwise.

IER. Of course you can. I can't come with you, but I shall be there in spirit.

IER. It's hard, I know; but you can and you must.

IEE. . . . I really don't know if I'll come again.

IER. Well, it's up to you, but I think you should. You've done very nicely today, and next time I'm sure you'll do even better.

IEE. I'll never get a job — the way I look.

IER. Not so fast there, young man. Rome wasn't built in a day. We've just begun to explore the possibilities, and you already want to throw in the sponge. Let's see now. . . .

IEE. (*sobbing*) It's just awful!

IER. I know . . . it's been pretty rough going. . . . Try to stop crying now. You'll feel much better tomorrow, and the world will look brighter.

IEE. She hates me; I have proof.

IER. Now stop this; your mother does love you. She herself has told me so. She means to be nice to you, and I know you want to try hard to be nice to her. I assure you everything will work out if we all just get in there together. She is willing, and so am I. You'll see. . . .

IEE. My legs will be alright, won't they? They must be. If they're not, I'm going to kill myself!

IER. Now, just relax. Everything will be alright. The doctors are doing everything they can, and you know that medicine today can perform miracles. You'll be O.K. I'm just sure you will be. As for . . . well, I know you didn't mean that. Everything will work out fine.

Often heavy reassurance, stressing conscience, borders on moralizing. It may suggest disbelief as well — as though the interviewer were saying, "You couldn't possibly" or "I can't believe you would." These leads will be discussed later.

Suggestion

Suggestion is a mild form of advice. Its overtones tend to be tentative and vague. In it the interviewer proffers a possible line of action. Suggestion does not demand compliance nor threaten the interviewee with rejection should he not follow it through. I am speaking of true suggestion, of course, not of masked command. Suggestion provides the interviewee with the interviewer's considered opinions but leaves him leeway to accept, refuse, or propose ideas of his own. Indeed its purpose may be to stimulate the interviewee to think and plan for himself. When this is the interviewer's sincere intention, suggestion communicates: "I think my idea is a good one and may work. It's up to you, of course, to decide." If clearly stated as suggestion and genuinely intended as such, it is open rather than closed, provisional rather than final. It is equal speaking to equal, one of whom may possess more information, knowledge, or experience but is not determined to force it on the other. Suggestion may be offered at the interviewee's request, or it may be unsolicited.

IEE. . . . I can't come up with anything else. Do you have any ideas?

IER. I was thinking that it might be helpful to take him out of nursery school for awhile and keep him at home so he could see just what you do with the baby, instead of imagining all sorts of things the way he has been doing.

IEE. I can't make up my mind whether to get married in the spring or to finish college first. You know what I mean. . . .

IER. I think I do and suggest you try to talk it over with Bob from your viewpoint. He might surprise you after all. Then when you come in next week, we can discuss it further. How does that sound to you?

IER. I have a suggestion to make if you'd like to hear it. It's just an idea I have, and I'll offer it for what it may be worth. If you took that job at the X company, which involves fewer hours, you might be able to take enough credits at night to finish in two years and yet be financially independent. You might even get a loan from the university. We here might have some work during the summer at our camp. I'm sort of thinking out loud. How do you feel about all this?

IER. My suggestion is to go in there and do it. You've been hesitating quite awhile, and we've looked into all of the angles. If you don't make up your mind soon, you'll miss the boat. They don't care about how you feel but about what you can do; and you can do it. So I suggest you get started. That's the way I feel, in any case.

Advice

Whether or not to give advice has been and remains a controversial issue, which, unfortunately, cannot be resolved here. Again it is a matter of personal philosophy. Advice, essentially, is telling someone else how to behave, what to do or not do. It may be offered directly or indirectly; nonthreateningly or as an ultimatum. It may be tendered because we really feel that this is what the interviewee should do in his own best interest or because we feel compelled to release ourselves from a difficult situation and the easiest way is to give "disinterested" advice. We may proffer it to fulfill our need to dominate or to satisfy his need to submit. Before looking more closely at advice giving, I want to relate a personal experience that occurred some years ago and to this day aids me in decisions concerning advice.

A woman once came to see me and began the interview by declaring: "I've consulted with many people and received lots of advice. I didn't like any of it, and so now I've come to you to see what you've got to say. My problem is. . . ." Because I am convinced that all of us give advice much more often than we realize and because this issue is a basic one in the helping interview, I want to outline my views regarding it. Let me begin by considering advice that has actually — or at least verbally — been requested by the interviewee. The first step, I believe, is not to comply immediately with the request but rather to discover what the interviewee himself thinks about the situation under discussion and what alternatives — if any — he has considered. When the woman in my story learned that I refused to play at her game, she eventually suggested herself the "advice" she had been waiting to hear from someone else. However limited may be the application of the lesson I learned that day, still I feel certain that when the interviewer is asked for advice, it is essential that he first of all enable the interviewee to identify and delimit the areas in which he seeks advice. The interviewee should be encouraged to verbalize his hopes and fears regarding these areas — in brief, to throw as much light as possible on his own situation.

"I wonder what alternatives you have been considering."

"I realize that you are terribly concerned about this. Perhaps if you can tell me the various alternatives you have considered and how you feel about them, we may be able to arrive at something that makes sense for you."

"I wonder if you have discussed this matter with other people and how you feel about what they had to say. Perhaps if we understand what you exclude, we may be able to come up with something positive."

"I feel that all of us can profit from advice only — if at all — when it falls on fertile soil, so to speak; if you can tell me more about your own thoughts on the matter, we may be able to come up with something fruitful for you."

Obviously, innumerable ways to express this exist, but the aim is always to gather all possible thoughts and feelings from the interviewee concerning the subject on which he wants advice. At times this alone is sufficient to enable him to reach a decision. At other times slight clarification on our part will lead to positive results. In the event that the interviewee cannot reach his own solution, at least we shall have obtained from him as much information as we are likely to receive. No one can benefit from advice unless it is meaningful to him, unless he understands it in terms of his own frame of reference, and until he has expressed himself sufficiently so that he can really listen to the advice he claims he wants. Only then can he look upon it as meant for him in his particular life space.

Now arises the question of whether I, the interviewer, feel I have the right on moral, professional, or simply human grounds to give advice. If I conclude that I do not, I should say so openly and clearly.

"It's hard for you to decide, but I feel I have no moral right to do it for you. These are your children, and the decision as to whether to leave them with your wife's parents or to stay with them is one, I'm afraid, you'll have to make on your own."

"This lies beyond my professional competence. All I can do is to recommend a qualified physician who may be able to give you sound advice. But even here, different doctors have different approaches; and my guess is that, ultimately, you will have to make up your own mind."

"What should I do in your place? Honestly I can't say. I've tried to understand how things seem to you, but I cannot say whether they would look like this to me if I were you. As you will have to live with your decision, I don't want to influence it unduly. I have a feeling, however, that we have not yet considered all the aspects of the home in X. . . ."

It is essential as well that the interviewer ask himself whether he has a need to give advice, in specific instances or generally. Such a need may interfere with the interviewee's struggle to decide what is best for him. The interviewer's need to advise may prematurely cut off the joint examination of the matter under discussion. If the interviewer can become aware of this need, he may think twice before giving advice and ask himself whether it has been solicited and whether it is, in fact, required.

I feel it is also important that the interviewer examine to what extent the interviewee feels he cannot decide alone. The interviewee may have learned to regard himself as someone who requires the advice of others, who is incompetent to choose, who must always be dependent on a "specialist." Am I then really helping by tendering the advice he seeks? May I not be reinforcing his negative concept of himself? Will he be able to build upon my advice, or will advice seeking lead to more advice seeking, dependence to more dependence? Does he possess the inner resources required to carry out someone else's advice, or will he ask for more in order to reinforce it? Would I possibly be of more assistance by withholding advice, by attempting to show him what is involved in his seeking it and enabling him to change his self concept?

When rapport is good and the interviewer is genuine, he can

allow himself to say to the other: "No, I will not solve your vocational dilemma for you. You seem to see yourself as a poor, unfortunate cripple, but I don't. If I were to tell you what to do, you would have a basis for thinking that I consider you one. Then there would be two of us with that opinion. I'd rather there be none, but if there must be one, it won't be me. So let's get down to business and consider what you ought to be doing with the rest of your life as far as work is concerned."

It is often easier to advise than to become more deeply involved in the struggles of another. This interviewer acted not from weakness but from strength. He did not take the easy way out, and his refusal to succumb was in the end justified.

Sometimes, especially when the contact is brief and superficial and we sincerely believe that we cannot help the interviewee effect a change in himself, it may seem unavoidable to give advice and be done with it. Unfortunately, many of us feel we must act in this manner at times. A stone wall confronts us, and all we have in the way of tools is a chisel.

IEE. You're the counselor here . . . you've got to know what my son should study. I don't know, and I don't care as long as it's an honest living. You're getting paid for giving advice. If I knew what school to send him to, I wouldn't waste my valuable time coming to you. I've got better things to do.

IER. Perhaps you'll let me discuss this matter of schools with your son. He may know in which direction. . . .

IEE. Oh no! You're going to tell me, and I'll tell him; and he'd better listen to me if he knows what's good for him.

Having weighed all these considerations, the interviewer must still ask himself a few final questions before, at long last, he provides the best advice he can. "Do I know enough about what is involved to give advice? Do I possess enough factual information, as well as sufficient knowledge of the expressed thoughts and feelings of the interviewee, so that my advice will be sound and meaningful for him? Have we arrived at the stage where my advice may truly aid him?" A single example will suffice.

IER. Well, I believe we have looked into this matter of housing for you and your family quite thoroughly. Considering everything you have told me and the housing situation as I know it, I feel that it would be best not to move at this point. This isn't an ideal solution for you, I know, and it will be particularly hard on Jim; but, on the other hand, you seem to feel sure that you can handle his school difficulties for another year. By then, things may have changed. . . .

Now that advice has been provided, how does the interviewee receive, understand, and react to it? In the above instance, Jim's mother felt the interviewer had put into words her own uncrystallized thoughts. The advice seemed sound to her, and they agreed to meet again the following year to consider what ought to be done then. If an interviewer gives advice within the framework delineated above, he will wish to elicit an open reaction to it. He may say: "I wonder how you react to this" or "It would be helpful to both of us if you would tell me what you really think of this advice. Since it is meant for you, it is important to know whether you feel it will be useful to you."

Occasionally interviewers fall into a trap. The interviewee seeks advice to prove that it is worthless and, by implication, that the giver is as well. If we are caught, it will not be because we have had no warning, and we shall have to devise our own means of escape. This reflection leads me to a more general consideration: How do we feel and react when our opinion, judgment, advice, are rejected? Do we take it as a personal affront, or can we cope with it? Do we perhaps even enjoy watching the interviewee make his own decision by tearing ours down? Do we thrust these "pearls" of ours upon him, or do we display them in order that he may examine them and decide for himself which, if any, to acquire for his own use?

How do we feel when our advice is accepted — and doesn't work? At least, the interviewee claims it doesn't work for him. Do we then have to defend our own wisdom, or do we seek to understand what is happening to the interviewee? What if our advice works for the interviewee and, glowing with gratitude, he returns and requests more advice, guidance, and direction?

We are so wise. Why not pour out just a little more of that profound wisdom? When we feel that this is a bit too much, whom do we blame, with whom do we become angry? We can resolve our doubts quite nicely by categorizing him as an ungrateful nuisance and a dependent being. We, of course, meant only to help, but some people, we tell ourselves, just take advantage. And that solves it — for us.

Those interviewers who insist on giving advice even when it is unsolicited, I have found, tend to be the ones who resent it most when the advice is rejected or misunderstood. Underlying the advice seems to be a kind of ultimatum: Take it or leave me. However, even if the interviewer has no need to control others, he may still find it necessary on occasion to offer advice not specifically requested. He may hit upon something the interviewee does not know, has not considered, or regards as out of the question for him. If he can offer such advice and not feel rejected should it be turned down, if he offers it deliberately, keeping the reservations referred to in mind, he will not be endangering the relationship.

IER. Have you ever considered becoming a professional photographer? You obviously like photography and spend a lot of time at it. In terms of your disability, this might work — and you might do for a living what you seem to enjoy doing as a hobby. Perhaps you want to think it over. We could discuss it when you come in next week. If you think of anything else, we could also discuss that.

One last word. When advice has been given, it should be followed up. I feel we should meet with the interviewee again or at least communicate in some way to ascertain to what extent our advice has proved helpful. If it has not aided, we may wish to explore the situation with the interviewee to learn what went amiss. This will provide an indispensable source of feedback for the interviewer interested in his professional growth and personal development. Also, it will indicate to the interviewee that advice giving is not necessarily the final stage in our relationship — unless he decides it should be because he no longer needs us. Should he wish to return and we have not left the door wide open, he may hesitate, fearing that we shall be displeased with the way he carried out the advice. We must convince him by our behavior that we are far more interested in him than in any advice we have given. More often than not, people accept advice and leave; and we never hear from them again. The advice may or may not have helped. In either event we should want to know. If we have left the door open, we can always continue where advice giving left off or start afresh. Closed doors constitute a barrier to further communication.

Urging

Urging, which is so closely related to persuasion and cajoling that I shall not try to differentiate between them, is a lead or response the purpose of which is to prod the interviewee, to not let him escape what, in our opinion, he should not evade. Urging involves supporting in order to strengthen the interviewee's determination to carry out whatever it is that both partners have discussed and the interviewer, at least, feels would be beneficial to the interviewee. It relates to the practical aspects of a theoretical discussion or agreement. For example, both may agree that the interviewee ought to resume his studies. This remains theoretical as long as the interviewee does nothing about it. The interviewer urges, cajoles, persuades, the interviewee to spur him into action, to turn theory into practice.

Frequently urging takes place after advice has been ostensibly accepted by the interviewee or at least has not been rejected outright. This is the very point at which urging may be dangerous. We have given advice in good faith and assume the interviewee has accepted it, but nothing further happens. He does not move to carry it out. So we urge, cajole, persuade. We build on what we believe to be the solid foundation of our advice without checking to see whether this foundation is of sand or stone. What is needed here is less urging and more examining of the life space of the interviewee. Perhaps this is his way of rejecting our advice. Perhaps this is his way of letting us know that theoretically the advice is sound but that practically, for him at least, it is irrelevant. This refusal to budge may well be his way of communicating that we must seek another alternative, one that will prove more meaningful for him.

Sometimes, I admit, urging has positive results. Ultimately, our support and belief in the interviewee may strengthen him sufficiently to enable him to act. Even in this event, I am certain that we must always check whether we are supporting and showing belief in the interviewee or in our own advice. Behind the interviewee's rejection of or resistance to our advice, expressed in hesitation or inaction, may just possibly glimmer the sparks of self-initiated action. By recognizing this tiny flame and kindling it, we give the most significant help of all.

In summary, I propose that when you discover that you are urging, take note of the effect this produces on the interviewee. Are you inadvertently forcing him to the wall? Are you urging *your* case, assuming it to be his as well? What is *his* case? What can you both learn from a situation in which a line of action theoretically agreed upon breaks down when the time comes to carry it out? Are you so engrossed in urging that you cannot see anything else, even the interviewee's attempt to come to grips with his own problem in his own way? Are you listening to him with all the understanding you can muster, or do you insist he listen to you and get moving? Following are a few illustrations:

IER. I thought we had agreed you would write that letter. Of course, talking about it won't get it written. You thought it such a good idea just a few days ago, and here you are, and the letter isn't written yet.

IEE. It was a good idea of yours and still is. I tried several times, but I tore them all up. They just weren't right. Perhaps I just can't do it.

IER. But of course you can. It needn't be a literary masterpiece. It just needs to be written. I have pen and paper right here. Why don't you try to write it now, while we're on the subject?

IEE. I just can't. I've been thinking things over, and . . . I thought it might be better, after all, to tell it to him in person. It'll be hard to say it; but since I can't write it, perhaps I have no other choice.

Here the interviewee proposed a course of action more meaningful to her. The interviewer, in spite of her initial urging, was able to listen and to pick this up. The two of them examined it together, and eventually the interviewer was able to support the interviewee in this course. The letter remained unwritten, but the conversation took place. Although it was far from satisfactory, still it was better than nothing. In time, more conversations followed between the interviewee and her estranged son. However, not all interviewees are as determined, nor are all interviewers as perceptive and as prepared to retreat in order to advance afresh. For example:

IER. Well, how did it go?

IEE. It didn't . . . I mean, I never showed up. It was very nice of you to make the appointment but . . . I just couldn't go.

IER. It wasn't easy to arrange that appointment for you. I really don't understand. After all, you agreed it would be best to see the head of the department, and so I went out of my way to get him to see you and now. . . .

IEE. I'm very sorry, but I just couldn't face up to it.

IER. Being sorry doesn't help us. He's an extremely busy man, and I don't know if I can arrange another appointment. However, I'll try. I'll let you know if and when he will see you. I won't give up and won't let you throw up your hands either. He's a nice man in his own way, and, in any case, he won't bite.

IEE. That's really very good of you; but on thinking it over, I've kind of given up the. . . .

IER. Well, one can't give up that easily. I won't, and you won't. It may be slightly embarrassing for me to explain — but I don't care. I'll get another appointment for you, and this time you'll go. Once you're in that office talking to him, you'll see that it isn't half as bad as you anticipate it to be right now. We've come so far, and we can't give up now.

IEE. I don't even know whether I want to work there. . . .

IER. Come on now — of course you want to work there; that's all we've talked about for weeks now. You're hesitating, but I'm not. Right now it seems difficult, but some day you'll appreciate all this. It took us such a long time to make up your mind in any direction that we must keep at this till we succeed. You'll see; it won't be bad at all, and once it's over you'll be all set.

The appointment was duly made; the interviewee did not appear. The interviewer thought he recognized irresponsibility, ingratitude, and lack of cooperation. The contact was broken off.

Below are two final examples of urging in which previous advice giving was not involved:

IEE. I could do homework at my friend's house.

IER. You could study there, but you don't.

IEE. I think my mother would be insulted — you know, like my house wasn't good enough for me, or something.

IER. We could check on that, but I'm sure your mother would be pleased with the arrangement. In our last talk she told me how hard it was for you to do homework with all the little ones around. As for studying at Bob's house, that might help Bob, too. You know it's hard for him to settle down before late in the evening, and this way both of you might profit.

IEE. Well, I never really tried it.

IER. Why don't you, and see how it goes? You could ask your mother, too, and let me know if I understood her correctly or not. If you try it this week, we could talk about it next week. Do you think you are going to try?

IEE. If Mother agrees, I'll try it.

IER. I really think you ought to. I'll see you next week.

Contrast the above example with the following:

IER. This is the setup at our center. It may seem rigid, but you must go through all the prescribed activities so that the instructors can evaluate your performance and determine what you are best suited for.

IEE. Yes, but so much of this stuff is childish and. . . .

IER. I can only urge you again to make the best of things. If instead of complaining you had gone ahead, by now you might already be done with the simpler tasks. No one wants to hold you back, but there are certain procedures. . . .

IEE. I think I could do better at. . . .

IER. If you would only conform, it would be to your best advantage.

Moralizing

Moralizing is a mixture of advice giving and urging with one significant addition. When the interviewer simply advises and persuades, he relies on his own judgment. For him, at least, this suffices. When he moralizes, however, he resorts to new weapons; he brings more powerful ammunition into action. He arrays these forces against the interviewee to make him "see the light." The main weapons the interviewer chooses are those two the interviewee will find most difficult to combat: conscience — his own, the interviewer's, or Everyman's; and morals — those sacred, social norms no one in his right senses could possibly oppose or even question.

The interviewee is trapped. To surrender is to admit defeat. To resist is to declare himself an outlaw. Shall he bend the knee or raise his head in challenge? Thus beleaguered, he may act in a number of ways, but the chances are it will be acting, pretense. What is really happening within himself he is sure to keep well hidden. The foe is too formidable, the pressure too great, for anything but playacting or evasion.

True, it may not always be playacting; the "culprit" may genuinely feel guilty and be shocked by his own behavior. Moralizing has been known to work. His head falls upon his breast; he is deeply sorry and admits defeat. The interviewer has triumphed. But has the interviewee really been helped? What has he learned from this experience that will enrich his life and stimulate change in a direction meaningful for him? I venture the guess that he has probably learned to be more careful in the future so that he will not get caught again; or to accept the fact that resistance against an enemy so powerful is hopeless and that hence the wisest course is to submit, or comply; to give up trying to find himself and, instead, study the foe and emulate him.

On the other hand, if the interviewee is genuinely indignant and refuses to submit, if, openly defiant, he challenges the foe to do his worst, what has he learned that will enable him to change in a worthwhile direction? Here experience tells me he has usually learned that the enemy is powerful indeed and that in order to survive he must become more powerful still. He must become shrewd to outwit him. He must become a master of strategy. He may seem to submit, temporarily disarming his opponent, at present personified by the interviewer, in order to strike out hard at the first opportunity. He may, on the contrary, not give an inch but hold his ground as well as he can, never getting close to his own self because he is too busy withdrawing, defending, attacking.

You may consider my outlook onesided and insist that moralizing is a useful agent in the helping interview at times. I shall not argue the point any further, but I must add one comment. Check and double-check, for appearances may be misleading. Do not be content with present words, but observe future behavior. If you have been victorious, examine at what price your victory has been won; if defeated, think again before you reject the interviewee as "hopeless." Moralizing can be overwhelming. At best, it helps the interviewee see how society judges him, how others look upon his behavior. At worst, it blocks examination of self and self-motivated action and stifles further expression of feelings and attitudes. It can result in insightless submission or stubborn defiance. In the following illustrations moralizing is utilized both as lead and as response:

IER. Helping your dad for a couple of hours in the afternoon really isn't such a terrible thing. Your sister takes care of the entire household, and you want to do your share, I'm sure. I know it's hard not to play with the other boys, but you'll feel much better if you carry your share of the burden. Life isn't always a bed of roses; and, believe me, lots of boys have it much harder than you. For your departed mother's sake I know you'll want to make the effort.

IEE. (*silence . . . tears . . . silence*)

IER. You should have let me know when you thought of giving up the job. Jobs aren't easy to come by, and other people gave their time and energy to find you this one. Anyone else in your position would be glad to have. . . .

IEE. No, they wouldn't. Just because I've got a disability doesn't mean I've got to put up with all that crap. I should have let you know. Maybe some sucker could take it, but I can't and I won't.

IER. You must learn to live with your handicap. Jobs you can do are hard to find. Anyway, it couldn't have been as bad as you say.

IEE. It was, but I should have let you know. I'm sorry about that.

IER. Being sorry doesn't help now.

IEE. What do you want me to do, get down on my knees? If you don't have another job, just say so.

IER. No, I don't have one right now; and, anyway, first I have to consider those who are willing to make a real effort. Call me next month, O.K.?

In closing, let me cite some even more extreme examples of moralizing:

IER. You'll just have to make do with the allowance. Others manage quite well. You yourself admit that you drink a "little" and smoke too much. Saying that you're nervous won't feed your family nor clothe them either. You'll just have to get control of yourself. Of course, you love your family. So you'll just have to make an effort to prove it — not to me, but to them. They'll respect you the more for it, and you'll feel less nervous.

IEE. (*silence*)

IEE. I don't like Mr. J. one bit. He yells all the time, and he's unfair. He even calls kids names.

IER. I don't understand how you can say something like that even if you feel it. Mr. J. has told me how much he likes you and how hard he tries to get you to behave. I think you really ought to be ashamed of yourself. With your attitude you won't get very far in this world. People try to help you, and you go around saying unkind things about them. I suppose you were just a little angry then and don't really mean it, do you?

IEE. (*silence*)

IEE. You don't know my mother. If she could, she'd get rid of me. She's ashamed of me and hides me whenever she can. I wish I were dead.

IER. Now stop that nonsense. You're making it all up. It isn't right to talk this way about your mother after all she has done and is doing for you. I'm really surprised, a smart boy like you. Doesn't your conscience tell you that you're wrong?

IEE. (*silence*)

AUTHORITY LEADS AND RESPONSES

Now we are about to discuss the last group of leads and responses in this survey. Here, too, I make no attempt to be exhaustive and merely point up some of the major leads and responses falling into this category. In this group the interviewer perceives his role in a specific light and acts accordingly. Before we consider these leads and responses, therefore, let me say a few words about the philosophy underlying the interviewer's perception.

As we have proceeded in this chapter, we have witnessed a gradual change of attitude on the part of the interviewer. Except for minor deviations, we have moved along a continuum until we have arrived at the present point in our discussion. Let us look back now and examine this continuum. Although relatively fluid, it starts from a position in which the interviewee is central throughout the interviewing process and gradually shifts to the opposite position, in which the interviewer emerges as the central figure.

At one end of the continuum, the interviewer sees the interviewee as responsible for himself, as his own authority over himself. The interviewer treats the interviewee as an equal; he listens to him, tries to understand him empathically, and accepts him as he is. The interviewer attempts to clarify, to describe rather than evaluate, the thoughts and feelings expressed by the interviewee. He does his best to eliminate communication obstacles and is ready to assist the interviewee to move in the direction of meaningful change. When the interviewer considers it potentially helpful, he, as an equal in the interviewing process and as a congruent human being (Rogers, 1951), expresses his own ideas and feelings. He does not impose these on the interviewee but presents them as coming from an interested participant. His concern is not whether his ideas and feelings are adopted but whether they can help the interviewee come to grips with those ideas and feelings within himself that will mobilize him in the direction he chooses.

As the picture gradually changes till finally the interviewer occupies the center of the interviewing stage, we reach the point where the interviewer, willingly and consciously, sees himself as the authority. He accepts responsibility for what occurs in the interview and behaves and acts accordingly. He defines his role as a helping one, but for him, to help means to guide, to instruct, and, if necessary, to coerce. Inasmuch as he is the superior in the interview, for what other purpose could he be there? His authority derives from his knowledge, his skills, and his position and must be openly employed for the benefit of the interviewee. He is clear about values. He, at least, knows right from wrong, good from bad, proper from improper, and says so in no uncertain terms. He may listen to the interviewee and does his best to understand him; but he knows that, sooner or later, he will have to act — and is prepared to do so. Once he has decided on the course to follow he does not hesitate to instruct the interviewee in which direction to move. As he perceives it, this is the help the interviewee came to get, and in all fairness it is up to him to provide it. There are shadings at this end of the continuum also, but, essentially, the attitudes and behavior of the interviewer reflect the philosophy here outlined. I have tried to describe the authority position without bias; but because it is alien to my personal philosophy, I may have overstated or understated it. (For more detailed treatment of this subject, consult the Supplementary Reading List at the end of this book.)

Having considered the philosophy underlying the authority position, we are ready to discuss those leads and responses which are based on the clear assumption that under normal circumstances the interviewer will be able to solve the interviewee's problem once he identifies it — provided, of course, that the interviewee is prepared to cooperate, listen when necessary, and obey when ordered to do so.

Agreement-Disagreement

Here the interviewer tells the interviewee whether in his opinion the latter is right or wrong. Having gathered enough information from the interviewee, as well as from other sources when necessary, and relying heavily on his own experience and background, he states his position. Taking for granted that his judgment is sound, he naturally wants the interviewee to treat it seriously. Here are some representative examples:

IEE. I still can't make up my mind. I wonder whether the test results can help me to decide. I still want engineering but. . . .

IER. All the data lead me to think that engineering is the right course for you. The test results, as well as everything else you have told me, indicate that you are on the right track. I am clear on that; but if you hesitate much longer, you may miss the boat for next year's registration.

IEE. Don't you think that being blind is just the worst thing that can happen to a person?

IER. Well, frankly, I don't. It's hard being blind, I agree. But being totally deaf or bedridden, for example, is much worse. You may find this hard to believe at this point, but with time you'll see I'm right.

IEE. . . . and I'm sure it wasn't only Hitler and his guys who were responsible for starting the war, and I can't see blaming the Germans for everything that went on.

IER. You are quite wrong there. As you get older and read more on the subject, you will understand this better.

IEE. Doctor, can I get up tomorrow? I so much want to.

IER. I agree. As a matter of fact, if you hadn't asked me, I would have told you to anyway. One hour out of bed tomorrow, O.K.?

IEE. You said you'd let me know today whether you agree or not.

IER. I've thought it over carefully, and I personally can't agree. I'm convinced you and John can work things out, and I'm prepared to help you as much as I can. That's only my opinion, of course, but there are years of experience behind it. You just think it over and let me know.

Approval-Disapproval

This is similar to agreement-disagreement. However, not the question of right or wrong but of good or bad is involved. The interviewer expresses a value judgment when, from his frame of reference, this seems appropriate. He evinces approval or disapproval of the interviewee's behavior, contemplated plans, or outlook on life.

IER. Have you finally made up your mind to enter the competition?
IEE. Uh, yes.
IER. That's fine. I wish you success.

IEE. Oh, . . . I took the job after all. . . . Began yesterday. It isn't bad.
IER. I'm very surprised to hear that. I thought we had decided to look around further. Something more suitable for you would surely have turned up; but since you have decided, there is nothing more to be said at this point.

IEE. Jack and I are going to open our own photography shop.
IER. Good; I'm glad. Jack is such a nice fellow. I'm sure you two will make a go of it. Now I'm ready to discuss the matter of the loan.

IEE. Yesterday after class Mrs. R. asked me again what was the matter. I decided to tell her, and I did. I'm so relieved to have gotten it off my chest.
IER. I'm not certain that was wise. We had agreed that I would talk to her first, to kind of prepare the ground. I hope, at least, that you were tactful.

IEE. The way I see it, if I work all summer and stop fooling around, I can earn enough to get the car and still get ready for the exams in the fall.
IER. That's wonderful. I was hoping that this is what you would decide. I'm sure you've chosen correctly; and as I told you, our agency is always glad to help fine boys like you.

Opposition and Criticism

Both opposition and criticism were either openly expressed or implied in some of the preceding interviewer leads and responses.

When the interviewer opposes, he is saying no to a contemplated course of action. When he criticizes, he unambiguously expresses his displeasure with the interviewee's "bad" conduct or "mistaken" action. The interviewer, from his vantage point, is certain that this opposition or criticism is well founded.

IEE. I wish all of you would stop picking on me!

IER. I don't like your tone of voice. I for one am not picking on you, as you put it. You've been rude ever since you came in here, but I've tried to overlook it. I've tried to stretch out my hand to you in friendship, but you keep slapping it down. I won't have any more of this. Now it's up to you.

IEE. I'd like to go down to the post office alone. I'm working well with my dog, and I want to get my own stamps.

IER. Sorry, but you can't. I appreciate your desire for independence, but in my opinion you just aren't ready yet. Two more days of hard practice, and I may be able to allow it. What stamps do you need?

IEE. . . . I want to come in late on Monday. I've something important to take care of in the morning. Anyway, till they get things set up in the workshop on Mondays, I wouldn't miss more than a couple of hours, and I could make it up.

IER. Sorry, Bob, that won't do at all. If everybody did that, there'd be no one here. When you get out into industry, you won't be able to come and go whenever you like. Whatever you have to take care of can't be so important that it must be done first thing Monday morning. What is it, by the way?

Disbelief

Disbelief does not necessarily imply that the interviewer suspects the interviewee is lying. It does assume that the interviewee's perception of a given situation is incorrect or distorted and that the interviewer, from his position, can detect this and present an undistorted, more objective view. When employing disbelief leads and responses, the interviewer may well intend to encourage the interviewee by showing him — even through the use of sarcasm, if necessary — that things cannot possibly be as bad as he describes them. The interviewer is convinced that he can interpret the point at issue more correctly than the interviewee and thereby help him move along in a direction that his distorted perception now makes difficult, if not impossible, to pursue. In brief, the interviewer informs his partner that he can evaluate the situation more soundly and authoritatively and that the interviewee would do well to be guided by him. Thus, for example:

IER. Never on you?
IEE. She calls on everyone else but never on me, I tell you.
IER. I just can't believe it. After all, you're in the class like everyone else. It just doesn't make sense, the way you see it.

IEE. . . . And I didn't close my eyes all night, Doctor.
IER. The night nurse tells me you slept quite soundly for awhile. Maybe you slept with your eyes open.

IEE. For the others, yes, but for me never a good word.
IER. Now, Tom, I just can't believe that. You just remember the scoldings and forget the praise. Your mother did say how sensitive you are to criticism and that you seem to take praise for granted. Perhaps if you would make a list for just a week, you would get a different picture of what really goes on in your home.

Ridicule

In intent, ridicule is related to disbelief; but the lead or response is sharper, more sarcastic. Here the interviewer condescendingly instructs the interviewee for the purpose of demonstrating how absurd he and his perceptions are. Ridicule is a form of teasing that aims at shaming the interviewee into behaving "sensibly" like "other people" — such as the interviewer. The interviewer assures his partner that he, too, will evaluate the situation in the same light once he rids himself of these absurd notions and ridiculous perceptions. It is as if the interviewer were saying: "Yes, I am deliberately making fun of you so that you may be able to shake yourself free of your silly conceptions and act in a manner beneficial to yourself. This you can do only if you see reality the way I see it." Contrast the following in terms of intent and interviewer personalities:

IEE. . . . I thought about going back to work all day. . . .

IER. Tried your skill at e.s.p. . . . Thought the shop might move right into your home, I see!

IEE. I couldn't just walk up to her and tell her I was sorry.

IER. Oh, of course not, she might have eaten you.

IEE. You gave me so many medicines, I can't remember to take them all.

IER. I suppose you would like me to call you up every hour on the hour to remind you which ones to take.

IEE. I couldn't practice walking yesterday because it rained most of the time.

IER. I understand. You might have melted; and if you ever get a job, you expect them to pick you up by cab when it rains.

IEE. I just couldn't let you know I wouldn't make it last week.

IER. Naturally. The phones were out of order, and the mail service doesn't function in this town.

Contradiction

"It isn't so. It is otherwise. This is how it is." That is what the interviewer is stating or implying when he uses contradiction as a lead or response. He is saying "no," "wrong," "bad," to what the interviewee has expressed. He is certain of his ground and lets the interviewee know and feel this. There are no possible doubts, no two ways of looking at things. He intends to guide the interviewee onto the "right" path. He even contradicts the interviewee's expressed feelings when these are "bad" or "misguided." For example:

IEE. I feel awfully warm in here.

IER. You couldn't; all the windows are wide open.

IEE. I really love him and want to marry him.

IER. You want to marry him because of his wealth and his social position. You may fool yourself, but you can't fool me.

IEE. There's only dopes in this school, and I want to get the hell out of here real fast.

IER. This is not a school for retarded children. As a matter of fact, most of the children are as smart as, if not smarter than, you.

IEE. I'm quite happy "wasting away" as you call it.

IER. I know you're not. You're just taking the easy way out. You're miserable and lonely. No one could be happy living the way you do.

Denial and Rejection

Of the leads and responses listed in this series, denial and rejection are the most extreme. The interviewer employing them rebuffs the ideas, thoughts, and feelings of the interviewee, and in so doing, he may well be rebuffing the interviewee himself. He is telling the interviewee that unless his thinking, his attitudes, his behavior, change, nothing can be achieved in the interview. Unless the interviewee can adapt himself to the interviewer's perceptions, he is unworthy of any more of the latter's time, undeserving of any more of his attention. The interviewee is made to understand that under prevailing conditions, he can neither be guided nor assisted. He must either change or go. The interviewer, confident of his rectitude, can proceed no further. Some examples:

IER. We've gone over and over this same point. You insist that you can't and that you have tried. I insist that you can and that you haven't really tried. It's senseless to continue this way. You can come back to see me if and when you have something new to report.

IEE. . . . and I hardly got started, just got my tools ready, when the foreman told me to pack up and get out. I didn't even open my mouth.

IER. I happen to know that foreman, and your story just isn't true. The other times I couldn't check, but here I could and did. You were arrogant, defiant, and uncooperative; and from what he told me, you said plenty that was completely uncalled for. I hope you can get a job, but it won't be through us. We're through.

IEE. You just don't know what it's like, walking with a cane or a guide dog. People stare and point at you like you were a freak or something. I'm going to use a guide — Mother is ready to do it — or else I'll stay at home.

IER. Well, if that's your attitude, we can't help you. But just remember that Mother won't be around forever and then — well, it's your problem.

OPEN USE OF INTERVIEWER AUTHORITY

We are now reaching the phase in which the interviewer makes open use of his authority. He assumes complete responsibility for what occurs in the interview and dominates the situation accordingly. He acts out his authority position, as it were, and by his overt behavior goads the interviewee in a direction that seems to him correct beyond question. He is the determining figure in the interviewing process. His attitudes are central, but he moves one step further: In addition to expressing these attitudes, he acts upon them openly and unambiguously, assuming that if the interviewee can be thus coerced, he may eventually be helped. He sees no other path available and adopts this one as a last resort. I shall not consider here those interviewers who base their interviewing mainly on the open use of authority. Rather, I shall confine myself to the discussion of these leads and responses as occasionally used — leaving to the reader the decision as to their appropriateness and beneficial value.

Scolding

When scolding, the interviewer interprets and evaluates the ideas, feelings, and actions of the interviewee. Having understood these to his own satisfaction, he reacts to them negatively. "This is no way to think or feel or act," he admonishes. The interviewee needs correcting; and in the hope that a verbal thrashing will do the trick he administers it without delay:

IEE. I thought the paper wasn't due till next week.
IER. I don't know whatever gave you that idea. Everyone else seems to have understood. You'd better think less and listen more. There's still time to write it, so get to work.

IEE. I know they're my parents, but I don't feel as if they are.
IER. You don't feel that they're your parents? What silly things

you come up with! We went all through this, and you said
yourself that you know they are. I know it's been hard; but it's
all over now, and you'd better get a hold on those feelings of
yours before they get a hold on you. So many children didn't
find their parents again; you're lucky that you did — right?

IEE. I'd rather you told him I want to change.
IER. Look here, Bill, you'd better stop that. You always want
others to do your work for you when it's unpleasant. The
pleasant things you're quite ready to do alone. We've talked
about this a lot, and I think you understand why you do it,
but understanding isn't enough. You have to act on what you
know. You'd better tell him yourself that you want to change
because I'm not going to do it for you. The time has come
for you to grow up. If you can't tell him that you want to
change from woodwork to metal, how will you ever get the
gumption to ask a girl to marry you? Go on; get moving!

IEE. I meant well.
IER. So what? Meaning well isn't doing well. You hurt her very
much, and I'm quite upset about the whole thing. Next time
you'd better think of others more and yourself less.

Threat

Through the use of threat, the interviewer notifies the interviewee of the steps he will take should the interviewee continue
along his present path. He says, in effect, that he will mobilize
the power at his command, which is, of course, much greater
than any the interviewee can muster. What this amounts to in
a broader, social context is that the interviewer warns the interviewee of the consequences awaiting him should he persist in
his erring ways. It is a distinct warning.

IEE. I'm telling you the truth. I didn't take those pencils!
IER. If you persist in lying, I'll have to turn you over to the principal, and he . . . well, he'll know what to do.

IEE. I couldn't help it; my bus came late again this morning.
IER. If you come late once again, we shall have to ask you to leave
our workshop. Maybe one bus came late, but I know there
was one before that which you could easily have caught.

IEE. I think my brother is just bad through and through.

IER. You just go on thinking like that and getting him to believe it, too, and your brother may wind up in jail yet; he may want to prove you right.

IEE. . . . even though I've got the grades and the scholarship, I just don't want to go to college now.

IER. If you keep this nonsense up, I'm going to tell your parents to give you up as a lost cause. You're not going to college for me; and if you don't go, you'll see how far you can get!

IEE. I don't feel as if we're getting anyplace.

IER. No surprise to me! With your attitude it's no wonder we aren't getting anywhere. We'd better stop, but if you honestly believe that you will get far in this world with the way you have of looking at things, you're greatly mistaken. Unless you change — and fast — you're heading for plenty of trouble.

Command

Here the interviewer unequivocally orders the interviewee to follow his instructions. He acts on the assumptions previously mentioned and, perhaps, this additional one: The interviewee needs to be marshaled by a firm hand, and he, the interviewer, is best qualified to accomplish this task.

IEE. . . . they just come. . . . I can't control my tears.

IER. Of course you can. Pull yourself together: wipe your eyes, and blow your nose. We have lots to talk about.

IER. Stop playing with your hair; it is too distracting.

IEE. I can't play ball today. My hand. . . .

IER. Get out on that field. I'll be out there, and I want to see you pitching as you've never pitched before.

IEE. I've got to see you today.

IER. You came an hour late for the last appointment, too. Get out now, please. I'm very busy, as you can see. You wait outside, and I'll tell you later when I can see you.

IEE. I really don't know if I should. . . .

IER. Get on that plane; and when it's all over, come in to see me

again. I don't want to see you till you've given this thing a
fair chance. I know you can do it, and you will, too. Good
luck!

Punishment

The interviewer, feeling he must chastise the interviewee for
some impropriety of deed or attitude, brandishes the power and
influence implicit in his role. He may even claim to be helping
the interviewee thereby, although the latter may not appreciate
this at the moment. Here the interviewer plays his last trump
on the premise that if it doesn't work, nothing will. Even
when this most authoritarian of approaches is resorted to, interviewer intent and attitude vary greatly. Contrast the following:

IEE. I broke his glasses. The others just watched.
IER. I'm glad you told me, Dick, although I already knew it. You'll
have to pay for them, you know. I can arrange work for you
in the cafeteria if you don't have enough money to pay.

IEE. All they do around here is give you the runaround.
IER. Then you'd better look for another agency. Good-bye.

IEE. You all just talk, but you're really afraid to do anything.
IER. Well, I for one am not. You're suspended from all activities
for a week, and you are not to leave the grounds, of course.

IEE. He's my child, and I'll do whatever I like with him.
IER. You are quite mistaken. The law, in such cases, protects the
child against his parents, and we'll go to court to enforce it.
I'll have to show you who is stronger, and I won't hesitate to
do it!

Humor

I find myself incapable of concluding on such a somber note.
Luckily for me, one more interviewer reaction deserves mention. I have often found that humor when appropriately used
can be as helpful as many other leads or responses, if not more
so. Although I cannot define exactly what I have in mind, I
definitely do not mean sarcasm, ridicule, or cynicism. Rather,
I am thinking of that light touch of humor which stems from

empathic listening and which reflects a positive outlook on life. It is a very individual and personal response, for which there is no detailed recipe. Sometimes it results in our spontaneously laughing with the interviewee; at other times, in our provoking laughter in him. Now and then it is an anecdote which fits the situation — one which, the interviewer believes, will produce no obstacle to communication but may serve to ease tension and lighten the atmosphere.

I am referring, of course, to spontaneous, not artificial, humor — something very natural, not contrived. It may well consist of no more than a raised eyebrow, a smile, a gesture. When it breaks through, it brings the two partners in the interviewing process closer together by establishing an additional bond. For lack of a better term, I can only call this bond genuine liking for each other and confidence in the helping nature of human rapport.

LEAVE-TAKING

When, at long last, I began putting this book down on paper after years of thinking about doing so, writing the introduction proved rather easy. Taking leave is more difficult. It is like something that occurs at times in the helping interview. When the time comes for the two partners finally to take leave of each other, they both know it is an ending, and so they linger awhile, no longer needing each other but enjoying their mutual reflections. So I find it hard to separate now, to go on my way. Not that I can't; indeed I must. But there is a desire to linger just another moment, to meditate on what has been accomplished and to consider how it has been done.

I have written this so that we might think deeply and dispassionately about the helping interview and do so with as many communication barriers as possible removed, including that of esoteric language. I wished us to consider the many ways in which interviewers behave and the influence their particular mode of behavior may have on the interviewee. Since there are practically as many modes of behavior as there are interviewers, I have tried merely to depict certain patterns that seem to me predominant. The interviewee himself remains the eternal question mark. We never know in advance who he will be; but whoever he is, we must always be prepared to try to help him.

The interviewer's behavior, I am convinced, strongly affects the interviewee's perception of him as a person and the interviewee's reaction to the interviewing process. If our behavior did not matter, there would be little point in writing about it. It does matter, however, and will as long as human beings try to help other human beings through the interview. Should nonhuman interviewers — computers — take over this function, my premise will no longer hold. I hate to contemplate the implications of such a change and return posthaste to the human interviewer, for whom I have written.

I believe that what is true for the interviewee is true for ourselves, the interviewers, as well. People can change; people do change. Without this conviction on our part, the interview, our tool, would disintegrate. The debate rages as to what brings change about — what promotes it and what hinders it. We can change our behavior if we can allow ourselves, first of all, to find out how we do actually behave. By analyzing our own behavior nondefensively, we can learn a great deal. No longer feeling threatened, we can permit ourselves to examine our work closely. Through the use of tapes, notes, observers, supervision, discussion, interviewee feedback, and self-examination, we can arrive at the point at which we are able to describe our behavior in the helping interview. Having described it, we can then consider whether this is, in fact, how we believed we were behaving and whether we wish to continue to behave thus. My hunch is that we shall always find a gulf — or at least a fissure — between what we are actually doing, what we thought we were doing, and what we ideally wish to do.

It is my conviction that we can change our behavior in the direction of our philosophy. In other words, we can change toward the self we wish to become. However, change involves arduous work, of the kind no one can perform for us. A pertinent book may aid us; so may a perceptive supervisor, notes, tapes, role-playing, and frank discussions with colleagues. Ultimately, change involves never-ending work that each one of us must perform within himself.

Our thinking about the helping interview does not remain static either. It, too, changes as we experiment and discover more about how our behavior affects that of others. As I ponder what I have written, I realize that I have not been as descriptive as I meant to be. Perhaps my own values have too often intruded. I can only repeat once more that my intention has been to stimulate thought and, possibly, change but that the direction this thought, this change, takes must be of your choosing.

When interviewing, we are left with what we are. We have no books then, no classroom lessons, no supporting person at our elbow. We are alone with the individual who has come to seek our help. How can we best assist him? The same basic issues will confront us afresh whenever we face an interviewee for the first time. In summary they are:

1. Shall we allow ourselves to emerge as genuine human beings, or shall we hide behind our role, position, authority?

2. Shall we really try to listen with all our senses to the interviewee?

3. Shall we try to understand with him — empathically and acceptingly?

4. Shall we interpret his behavior to him in terms of his frame of reference, our own, or society's?

5. Shall we evaluate his thoughts, feelings, and actions and if so, in terms of whose values: his, ours, or society's?

6. Shall we support, encourage, urge him on, so that by leaning on us, hopefully he may be able to rely on his own strength one day?

7. Shall we question and probe, push and prod, causing him to feel that we are in command and that once all our queries have been answered, we shall provide the solutions he is seeking?

8. Shall we guide him in the direction we feel certain is the best for him?

9. Shall we reject him, his thoughts and feelings, and insist that he become like ourselves or at least conform to our perception of what he could and should become?

These are, as I see them, the central issues. How we meet them today need not be the way we shall meet them tomorrow. The choice is ours.

SUPPLEMENTARY READING LIST

(Books referred to in text are preceded by an asterisk. The comments that follow some of the listings are by Alfred Benjamin.)

A. General surveys of interviewing

Bingham, W., and Moore, B. *How to Interview*, 4th ed. Harper, 1959.

Kahn, R., and Cannell, C. *The Dynamics of Interviewing*. Wiley, 1957.

> Both books consider, in brief, all aspects of interviewing. I prefer the latter because it is more oriented to the helping interview; see especially Chapters 1 and 2.

B. Books, including casebooks, dealing specifically with the helping interview

Bordin, E. *Psychological Counseling*. Appleton, 1955.

> An eclectic clinical approach.

Brammer, L., and Shostrom, E. *Therapeutic Psychology*. Prentice Hall, 1965.

> See especially Chapter 7.

Buchheimer, A., and Balogh, S. *The Counseling Relationship*. Chicago: Science Research Associates, Inc., 1961.

> Very useful casebook with a clearly defined outlook.

Callis, R., *et al.* *A Casebook of Counseling*. Appleton, 1955.

Evraiff, W. *Helping Counselors Grow Professionally*. Prentice Hall, 1963.

> I recommend this very highly because the interviews included are analyzed by several specialists from divergent viewpoints.

*Fenlason, A. *Essentials in Interviewing.* Harper, 1952.

Parts II and III are extremely relevant.

Garrett, A. *Interviewing: Principles and Methods.* Service Association of America, 1942(58).

An introductory "must."

Miller, L. *Counseling Leads.* Pruett Press, Boulder, Colo.

Patterson, C. H. *Counseling and Psychotherapy: Theory and Practice.* Harper, 1959.

Very much in line with my own approach.

Patterson, C. H. *Theories of Counseling and Psychotherapy.* Harper, 1966.

Porter, E. H., Jr. *Therapeutic Counseling.* Houghton Mifflin, 1950.

Indispensable for purpose of interviewer self-examination whether or not one accepts his nondirective approach. See especially "Pre and Post Tests."

Rogers, C. R. *Counseling and Psychotherapy.* Houghton Mifflin, 1942.

Classic statement of the nondirective point of view.

Sachs, B. *The Student, the Interview, and the Curriculum.* Houghton Mifflin, 1966.

Snyder, W. *Casebook of Non-directive Counseling.* Houghton Mifflin, 1947.

*Sullivan, H. S. *The Psychiatric Interview.* Norton, 1954.

Although not directly applicable, this book is most thought-provoking for the student of the helping interview.

Thorne, F. C. "Directive and Eclectic Personality Counseling," *Six Approaches to Psychotherapy,* eds. J. McCary and D. Sheer. Holt, 1955.

The authoritarian position par excellence.

Tyler, L. F. *The Work of the Counselor,* 2d ed. Appleton, 1961.

See Chapters 2 and 3, which are well worth reading and rereading.

Williamson, E. G. *How to Counsel Students.* McGraw-Hill, 1939.

Williamson, E. G. *Counseling Adolescents.* McGraw-Hill, 1950.

This author leans toward the authoritarian approach. Both works deserve perusal.

C. *Books and articles dealing with the philosophy of the helping interview and miscellaneous books mentioned in text*

Arbuckle, D. *Counseling: Philosophy, Theory and Practice.* Allyn and Bacon, 1965.

An outstanding exposition of the client-centered philosophy.

*Beck, C. E. *Guidelines for Guidance.* William C. Brown, Iowa, 1966.

Treats all the major contemporary philosophical approaches. See especially Chapter 48 by E. Dreyfus.

Boy, A., and Pine, G. *Client-centered Counseling in the Secondary School.* Houghton Mifflin, 1963.

*Buber, M. *I and Thou.* C. Scribner's Sons, 1952.

Buber, M. *The Knowledge of Man.* Harper & Row, 1965.

See especially "Appendix: Dialogue between Martin Buber and Carl R. Rogers."

*Bugental, J. F. *The Search for Authenticity.* Holt, 1965.

A well defined existentialist approach.

*Coleman, J. C. *Abnormal Psychology and Modern Life,* 3d ed. Scott Foresman, 1964.

*Fiedler, F. E. "The Concept of an Ideal Therapeutic Relationship," *Journal of Consulting Psychology,* Vol. 14 (1950), pp. 239–245.

*Fiedler, F. E. "A Comparison of Therapeutic Relationships in Psychoanalytic, Non-directive and Adlerian Therapy," *Journal of Consulting Psychology,* Vol. 14 (1950), pp. 436–445.

*Fiedler, F. E. "Factor Analyses of Psychoanalytic, Non-directive and Adlerian Therapeutic Relationships," *Journal of Consulting Psychology*, Vol. 15 (1951), pp. 32–38.

*Freud, A. *The Ego and the Mechanisms of Defense*. International Universities Press, 1946.

*Freud, S. *Little Hans*. Hogarth, 1955.

*Freud, S. *The Problem of Anxiety*. Norton, 1936.

Freud begins and his daughter elaborates the study of defense mechanisms.

Heller, K., *et al.* "The Effects of Interviewer Style in a Standardized Interview," *Journal of Consulting Psychology*, Vol. 30 (1966), pp. 501–508.

*Jourard, S. M. *The Transparent Self*. Van Nostrand, 1964.

Jung, C. G. *Modern Man in Search of a Soul*. Harcourt, 1932.

See especially Chapter 11.

*Lewin, K. *A Dynamic Theory of Personality*. McGraw-Hill, 1935.

Theoretical discussion of "life space."

*Maslow, A. *Motivation and Personality*. Harper, 1954.

Discusses coping as opposed to defense.

Maslow, A. *Toward a Psychology of Being*. Van Nostrand, 1962.

Matarazzo, J. D., and Wiens, A. N. "Interviewer Influence on Durations of Interviewee Silence," *Journal of Experimental Research in Personality*, Vol. 2 (1967), pp. 56–69.

May, Angel, and Ellenberger, eds. *Existence: A New Dimension in Psychiatry and Psychology*. Basic Books, 1958.

May, R. *Existential Psychology*. Random, 1961.

May, R. *Psychology and the Human Dilemma*. Van Nostrand, 1966.

McDaniel *et al. Readings in Guidance*, 2d ed. Holt, 1965.

McGowan and Schmidt. *Counseling: Readings in Theory and Practice*. Holt, 1962.

The above two collections of readings contain a rich and varied sampling of philosophical approaches.

*Reik, T. *Listening with the Third Ear.* Farrar Strauss, 1954.

*Robinson, F. *Principles and Procedures in Student Counseling.* Harper, 1950.

*Rogers, C. R. *Client-centered Therapy.* Houghton Mifflin, 1951.

*Rogers, C. R. *On Becoming a Person.* Houghton Mifflin, 1961.

See particularly Chapters 3 and 17.

Truax, C. B. "Reinforcement and Nonreinforcement in Rogerian Psychotherapy," *Journal of Abnormal Psychology,* Vol. 71 (Feb., 1966), pp. 1–9.

*White, R. W., ed. *The Study of Lives,* Essays on Personality in Honor of Henry A. Murray. Atherton Press, 1963.

See Chapter 8, "The Coping Functions of the Ego Mechanisms," by Theodore C. Kroeber.

Wiens, A. N., *et al.* "Speech Interruptions During Interviews," *Psychotherapy: Theory Research and Practice,* Vol. 3 (1966), pp. 153–158.

*Wright, B. *Physical Disability: A Psychological Approach.* Harper, 1960.

Analyzes coping vs. succumbing.